OH   HO

This book belongs to

Sasha Dresser

OH yay

Bible
Stories

Retold by Vic Parker

Miles
Kelly

First published in 2016 by Miles Kelly Publishing Ltd
Harding's Barn, Bardfield End Green, Thaxted, Essex, CM6 3PX, UK

2 4 6 8 10 9 7 5 3 1

Publishing Director Belinda Gallagher

Creative Director Jo Cowan

Editor Carly Blake

Designer Michelle Cannatella

Cover Designer Jo Cowan

Consultant Janet Dyson

Production Elizabeth Collins, Caroline Kelly

Reprographics Stephan Davis, Jennifer Cozens

ISBN 978-1-78617-172-6

Printed in China

British Library Cataloguing-in-Publication Data

A catalogue record for this book is available from the British Library

ACKNOWLEDGEMENTS
The publishers would like to thank the following artists
who have contributed to this book:
Cover: Scott Wilson (Advocate Art)
Inside pages: Katriona Chapman, Dan Crisp,
Giuliano Ferri, Mélanie Florian (The Bright Agency);
Andy Catling, Alida Massari, Martina Peluso (Advocate Art);
Aurélie Blanz

Every effort has been made to acknowledge the source and copyright holder of each picture. Miles Kelly Publishing apologises for any unintentional errors or omissions.

Made with paper from a sustainable forest

www.mileskelly.net

CONTENTS

The Old Testament 8-189

The Old Testament is the name for the first section of the Bible, made up of thirty-nine books written over two thousand years ago. They were compiled by Jewish people who lived in the Middle East (where parts of Israel, Palestine, Lebanon, Syria, Jordan, and Egypt are today). The books describe the Jews' special relationship with God over hundreds of years, beginning with the creation of the world. The Jews made many careful copies of the original ancient manuscripts, so the writings of the Old Testament were never lost. They contain family trees, religious laws, poetry, hymns, and stories that narrate the events of hundreds of characters.

The New Testament 190-191

The New Testament is the name for the second section of the Bible, made up of twenty-seven books. It describes the birth, life, and death of a man called Jesus, His teachings about God, and His followers. Jesus lived two thousand years ago in the Middle East. At that time, the Romans controled these lands and the Jewish people who lived there were unhappy about it. They were waiting for a savior—the "Messiah"—who would establish a mighty kingdom for them. The New Testament was written by the followers of Jesus, who believed Him to be the Messiah, during the one hundred years after He died.

INTRODUCTION

The Bible is often described as the world's best-selling book, however it is more like an entire library. It is made up of sixty-six individual books, and split into two sections known as the Old Testament and the New Testament. The Bible is believed by countless readers all over the world to be the Word of God. It was written by many people over more than one thousand years, from about 1450 BC. Originally written in Hebrew, Aramaic, and Greek, the Bible has been translated into many different languages.

The books contain detailed historical information, ancient proverbs and laws, songs, poetry, personal letters and diaries, stirring adventures of heroes and heroines, and marvelous tales of miracles and mystery. These writings teach us all about God, while entertaining and delighting us at the same time. Many captivating Bible characters and their colorful stories have become lifelong favorites of millions of children. We hope that the wonderful tales retold here will become yours, too.

Story Categories

The stories are divided into six different categories, or groups. Each group has its own icon, or symbol, which can be seen at the top of the pages. For example, if you want to read stories from the Mysteries and Marvels category, look for the pages with the yellow sun icon.

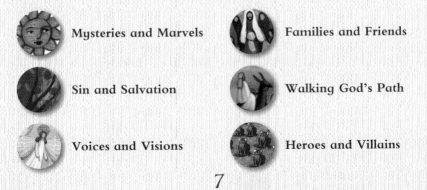

Mysteries and Marvels

Families and Friends

Sin and Salvation

Walking God's Path

Voices and Visions

Heroes and Villains

THE OLD
TESTAMENT

The Creation
of the World

In the beginning, God lived in darkness. There was nothing else except for a vast ocean that lay beneath. Then God had an idea. "Let there be light!" He said, and mysteriously there was. God liked the brightness. He enjoyed it for a while and then called the darkness back for another turn. That was the very first day and night.

When God lit up the second day, He had another idea. "I want a roof to arch over everything, way up high!" He said, and all at once there was one. Then He parted the ocean, scooped up half of the water, and poured it out onto the roof. The swirling patterns that formed above were beautiful. God gave the roof a special name—sky.

God looked down at the remaining water boiling and bubbling below. "Move aside so the land can show through!" He ordered, and it did. The land rose up and the water swirled around it. God was very pleased and decided to call them earth and sea. But He thought the land looked too bare. God imagined grass and flowers and bushes and trees. Before the third day ended, they were growing all over the earth.

On day number four, God decorated the sky. In it He hung a blazing, hot light called the sun, a pale, cold light called the moon and millions of burning, twinkling stars. Then He set them all moving around each other in a way that would mark out the passing of the days, nights, seasons, and years.

Next, God looked over His creation and decided that He wanted things to live in it. He spent the fifth day imagining all sorts of creatures that floated, swam, and dived in the water, and that soared, hovered, and buzzed in the air. Suddenly, the sea was filled with fish and sea creatures and the air

was busy with birds and insects.

On the sixth day, God imagined creatures that galloped, hopped, and slithered. Creatures with fur, scales, and shells, and with claws, hooves, and horns. Creatures that barked, hissed, howled, and grunted. All at once, the earth was alive with all kinds of animals.

Last of all, God took a handful of earth and modeled it into a figure that looked just like Him. He bent down and breathed into the figure's nostrils. It shivered, blinked, and came alive, and looked at Him. It was the first man, Adam. God quickly realized that the man would be lonely all on his own, so He sent him into a deep sleep while He made him a companion. God gently took out one of the man's ribs and healed up the wound. Then He shaped the rib into another, similar figure—the first woman, Eve. Finally, God brought Eve to life, then woke up Adam and introduced them to each other. God watched His two humans with delight as they spoke and got to know each other. God was so thrilled with them that He put them in charge of all the other living things He had made. He even planted a beautiful garden especially for Adam and Eve to live in, in a place called Eden.

At last, God sat back and looked at the world He had created. He had used every color, shape, and texture, and every size, sound, and scent that He could think of. God was very pleased with everything, and decided that He had done enough. He spent the seventh day relaxing after all His efforts. God ordered that from then on, every seventh day should be a special day of rest in memory of when He had completed His wonderful work.

And that is how the world was made.

Genesis chapters 1, 2

Adam and Eve in the Garden of Eden

God made sure that the Garden of Eden had everything that Adam and Eve needed to be happy. The sun kept them warm, so they didn't need clothes—they weren't embarrassed about being naked anyway. A gushing stream gave them water. All sorts of flowers, plants, and trees grew

there, fragrant and shady, and
bearing tasty fruits, nuts, and seeds.
In the middle of the garden grew
the two most beautiful trees of all—the
Tree of Life and the Tree of Knowledge.

"Take care of my marvelous garden,"
God told Adam and Eve. "Enjoy eating
anything you like, except for the fruits of
the Tree of Knowledge. Please do not eat
those. If you do, you will die."

Adam and Eve did as they were told and
their life in the garden was wonderful, until
one day Eve met a snake. The snake was by
far the most cunning of all the creatures
God had made. Very slyly, it asked Eve,
"Did God really tell you not to eat from
one of the trees?"

"Yes, that one," replied Eve, pointing to the Tree of Knowledge. "He said that if we do, we'll die. I don't think we're even allowed to touch it."

"Nonsense," hissed the snake. "You won't die! God doesn't want you to eat that fruit because if you do, you'll become like Him. You'll know the difference between good and bad, just as He does."

Eve gazed nervously at the Tree of Knowledge. How beautiful it was! Its leaves whispered mysteriously in the breeze and its branches stretched toward her. Its fruits hung down, ripe and ready to drop into her hand. "How wonderful it would be to become wise!" Eve murmured. Overcome with longing, she reached out, picked the nearest fruit, and took a big, juicy bite. It was so delicious! Surely something that tasted so good could not be wrong. Eve hurried to share the fruit with Adam and he couldn't resist trying it either.

Suddenly, Adam and Eve realized that they did indeed know the difference between good and bad—and what they had done was very wrong. The couple felt dreadfully ashamed and were embarrassed about being naked too. They tried to sew leaves together to cover themselves. Then, in horror, they heard God coming. Quickly, they hid, but God knew.

"Adam," God called, "why are you and Eve hiding from me?"

The red-faced couple crept out, hanging their heads.

"We were frightened when we heard You, and also we weren't dressed," Adam mumbled.

"What has made you want clothes? And why are you afraid of me?" God demanded. "You haven't eaten the fruit I asked you not to eat, have you?"

Adam owned up, but he blamed it all on Eve, who in turn blamed the snake. God listened as they squirmed and squabbled. Then with huge disappointment He said, "I have no choice but to punish you all."

He sent the snake crawling away in the dust, the enemy of humans forever. After making animal-skin clothes for Adam and Eve, He turned them out of their beautiful garden home. "From now on, you will have to fend for yourselves and struggle to grow food," God told them. "And one day, you will go back to being the earth from which I made you—you will one day die." He set angels with fiery swords to guard the Tree of Life, so that Adam and Eve could not eat its fruit to save themselves from eventually dying. God watched in great sadness as the shamed couple walked out into the world.

Genesis chapters 2, 3

The World's
First Crime

After Adam and Eve had been cast out from the Garden of Eden, their life was hard and harsh. However God made sure it wasn't always struggle and sorrow. In time He sent the couple children and they were overjoyed. The first baby born to Eve was a little boy whom they called Cain. Their

second was also a boy, whom they named
Abel. Both sons grew up to be healthy,
strong, and hardworking. Cain became a
farmer, while Abel chose to be a shepherd.
However the two brothers had very
different personalities. Abel was
goodnatured, kind, and caring, but his
brother Cain was bad-tempered.

Things came to a head one day when
Cain and Abel paid their respects to God.
They each prayed and
offered Him a gift.
Abel selected the
finest and fattest of
his sheep for his offering to
God, and Cain delivered
the very best of his crops

and fruit. God was very pleased
with Abel, but He not only
turned down Cain's offering,
He also told him off.

Instead of being
ashamed, Cain was furious
and his face looked like thunder.

"Why are you so angry? And why
have you got that scowl on your face?" God
demanded. "If you behave well, of course
I'll be happy to accept your offerings."

Cain stomped off, totally fed up with
God and burning with jealousy of his
younger brother. He could have thought
about what God had said and tried to turn
over a new leaf—but he didn't. Instead, He
allowed himself to be swallowed up by

anger and hatred and all he could think of was hurting his brother.

Cain plotted how to do this. He invited Abel to go with him to some distant fields deep in the countryside, where they were all alone. There, Cain suddenly turned on his younger brother in a vicious attack and soon Abel was lying dead on the ground.

Cain coolly returned home as though nothing had happened. He was sure that no one had seen him and that he would get away with his terrible crime, but of course God knew everything that he had done.

"Cain, where is your brother?" God challenged.

"How do I know?" Cain replied rudely. "I am not my brother's keeper."

Then God boomed, "Cain, what have you done? I can see your brother's blood staining the earth red. It is crying out to me, telling of your dreadful deed! From now on, the earth will not grow anything for you ever again. I am sending you to live far away, where I no longer have to look at you. You can wander homeless for the rest of your days!"

Cain fell to his knees in despair. "Please, God," he sobbed. "That's a terrible punishment. Not only are you driving me from my home and all that I know, you are sending me to certain

27

death. If strangers find me, wandering hungry and helpless, they're bound to kill me."

But God had had enough of violence and murder. He put a special mark on Cain that commanded that no one hurt him. Then God sent him away, far beyond Eden, to a distant eastern land called Nod.

Poor Adam and Eve had lost their first two children, but God took pity on them once more. He sent Eve other babies, beginning with a third son, Seth. And so the couple were comforted, and lived to such a great old age that they had the happiness of seeing many generations of grandchildren born to them.

Genesis chapter 4

Noah and the Ark

As the years went by, Adam and Eve's many great-great-grandchildren had many great-great-grandchildren of their own. People spread all over the world. They quite forgot that they were part of one big family. They also forgot about God and began behaving badly in all sorts of ways.

God looked down from Heaven and became more and more sad and angry. Eventually, people became so selfish and cruel that God was sorry He had ever created the human race. He decided the best thing was to remove everybody and start all over again.

Well, not quite everybody. There was just one person in the world who tried to live a good, honest, hardworking life—a farmer called Noah. God decided to save Noah, his wife and three sons, Shem, Ham, and Japheth, and their wives.

God spoke to Noah and told him about His terrible decision. "Look around you, Noah. Everyone in the world is evil, and I have had enough. I am going to wash everybody off the face of the earth, but I promise, you and your family will be safe. Here's what you have to do. I want you to build a huge, covered boat—an ark. Use the best wood you can find and build it 450 feet long, 70 feet wide and 40 feet high, with a roof of reeds. Coat the whole thing with tar, inside and out, so it is watertight. Give it a door and windows and build three decks divided into compartments. When I tell you, load up the ark with one pair of every living creature—a male and a female. Take seven pairs of animals you can eat because you will need enough food to feed you all. I am going to send forty days and forty nights of rain to flood the whole world."

Noah told his family and they hurried to begin the enormous task. Their neighbors thought they were mad as they began building the huge ship. How people laughed! But Noah and his family trusted God and kept working, and after many months the ark was finished. The day came when God warned Noah to begin loading the animals into the ark and settling his family onboard. A week later, thunder clouds blackened the skies, blotting out the sun, and it began to rain.

Genesis chapters 6, 7

The Great Flood

The rain that God sent to flood the world was like nothing anyone had seen before or could have imagined. It was as if the sky had shattered and through the cracks plunged mighty waterfalls. As the rain poured down, rivers burst their banks, lakes flooded their valleys, oceans swelled and overflowed, and the ark floated off on the rising waters. Towering tidal waves rushed over the land, drowning everything in their path and still the rain continued. The ark was lashed and battered, and hurled this way and that by the currents.

The rain fell for forty days and nights just as God had said. Then as quickly as it had started, it stopped. When Noah dared to peep out, he could see nothing but water in all directions.

Over the quiet, empty days that followed, the sun began to dry up the water and the flood gradually started to sink. God sent a great wind to speed things along. Eventually, the ark groaned and shuddered as it scraped along the ground and came to a halt on top of Mount Ararat in Turkey.

Noah didn't dare leave the ark yet. He waited a few days for the waters to sink further, then sent a raven into the sky. The raven soared back and forth and all it could see was water. Noah waited a week, then sent out a dove. It flew back the same day and Noah knew that there was not enough land showing yet. He waited another week, then sent the dove out again. That evening it returned, carrying an olive leaf. The waters were low enough to show land where trees grew! Noah waited one week more and again sent out the dove. This time it did not return. Nervously, Noah opened the door

35

and the ark was surrounded by dry land!

Then God called, "Noah, it's time for you and your family to go out into the world with the creatures and begin again." And that's what they did. God was pleased and blessed Noah and his family. He vowed that He would never again send a flood to destroy the living things He had created. God set a rainbow in the sky as a sign to always remind everyone of His promise.

Genesis chapters 7 to 9

The Tower of Babel

In the early days of the world people lived much longer than they do now. The Bible says that Noah was six hundred years old at the time of the flood and that he didn't die until he was nine hundred and fifty! Noah lived to see his sons and their wives have many children, grandchildren, and

generations of great-grandchildren. The
family grew so big that there were many
thousands of people in the world again, just
as God had wished.

Of course, people traveled to distant
lands to find places to live. Many spent
years wandering about, looking for good
grazing land for their animals, living in
tents that they moved from place to place.
As time went on, people in different lands
developed different tastes in clothing,
cooking, and customs, just like today. But
one thing they all had in common was the
same language.

When one particular group of wanderers
arrived at the land of Shinar, which is now
called Iraq, they decided to settle on a wide,

flat plain there. The countryside had everything the travelers could want, and they liked it so much that they decided they would never move on again. The travelers thought hard and came up with a big, bold plan. Instead of living in tents, they would build a lasting home for themselves—a fixed settlement made out of bricks.

They worked out how to make bricks from mud, which they could bake hard and stick together with tar. But the people didn't want to build just a village or a town, they didn't even want to build a city. They wanted to build the grandest, most beautiful city with a tower for a showpiece. A tower so tall that its top would touch the clouds. The settlers wanted news of their magnificent tower and spectacular city to spread far and wide, so they would become known throughout the world. Dreaming of fame and fortune, they began to build.

With all the digging, molding, baking, hammering, and chiseling that was going on, it wasn't long before God noticed what the people of Shinar were doing. He looked down from Heaven and was amazed at the pleasing streets that were being laid out, the stylish houses that were taking shape, and the stunning tower that was soaring upward into the sky. "My goodness!" God said to Himself. "I can't believe what these people are achieving! They're doing a wonderful job." But then a thought struck Him. "Hmmm… the only thing is, they're doing it because they want to be more important than everyone else. If I let them continue like this, they'll get quite carried away. Soon they'll want everything they have to be the biggest and best. I'd better put a stop to it before things get out of hand."

All at once, God gave the people different languages. Suddenly, they all found that they couldn't understand a word each other was saying. Without being able to communicate, their building plans ground to a halt. They couldn't work together to finish the city, which came to be known as Babel, or Babylon, because of the babble of voices inside it. Gradually everyone left Shinar in frustration and went their separate ways, seeking new homes.

From then on, as they settled in distant lands, people in different countries have spoken different languages.

Genesis chapter 11

43

Abram's Journey

One of the descendants of Noah's son Shem was a man called Abram. He grew up in a city called Ur, near the Persian Gulf. After Abram married he took his wife, Sarai, his father, Terah, and his orphaned nephew, Lot (whom he had brought up as his own son) to live in a northern city called

Haran. Both Ur and Haran were bustling places full of wealthy people just like Abram, who was a successful businessman. But one day, out of the blue, Abram heard God calling him.

"Abram, I want you to leave and go to the country that I will show you. I am going to make you the father of a great race of people."

It must have taken a lot of faith to do as God asked. Abram sold most of his possessions, packed up the rest, and set off with his wife on a long journey without really knowing where he was going. Abram did it without questioning and talked Lot into coming too. He bought flocks of sheep, goats, and cattle for himself and his

nephew. He hired shepherds too, and
bought camels and mules to carry tents,
belongings, food, and water. After weeks of
preparation, Abram led his family and
hired helpers away from everything they
knew, moving in a huge train south.

God led Abram down into the
land of Canaan, which is now
called Israel.
When Abram
reached

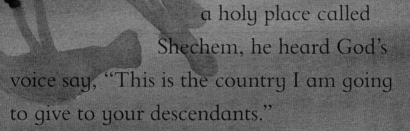

a holy place called
Shechem, he heard God's
voice say, "This is the country I am going
to give to your descendants."

Descendants! Abram was mystified. He
and his wife Sarai were well past middle-
age and although they had always longed
for a family, they had never been able to
have children. Again, Abram tried not to
question God, but to trust once more.

They could not stay in Canaan as there was a terrible famine, so God guided the family through the desert to the lush land of Egypt. Here, food and water were plentiful but Abram found himself in quite another kind of trouble. Pharaoh, the king of Egypt, ordered that Sarai had to become one of his wives. So God sent a terrible disease to strike Pharaoh and his advisors until he changed his mind, and he soon let Sarai go.

After that, Abram left Egypt behind and headed north into Canaan again to a place called Bethel. There wasn't enough grassland for all the animals to graze on, and Abram's and Lot's shepherds began quarreling and fighting over it. There was only one thing for it—the two men split up.

Lot went east into Jordan where he settled at a city called Sodom, while his uncle unpacked his tents and stayed in the countryside of Canaan. After Lot had left, God spoke to Abram again and repeated his vow. "Look around you," He said. "All this land as far as the eye can see will belong to you and your family forever."

And so Abram waited… and waited… Seasons came and went, but there was still no sign that he and Sarai would ever have children.

Over the years, God spoke to him several times, repeating his promise. It was always when Abram least expected it. One night, Abram was sitting outside his tent as usual when he heard God say, "Look up. You will have as many descendants as there are stars in the sky." Another time, after Abram had made an offering to God, he had a terrifyingly real dream. In it God walked right next to him, vowing again that he would have a vast, wealthy family and that all the land from the River Nile to the River Euphrates would be theirs.

As time went on, Sarai grew concerned that she would never be able to give Abram a child so she encouraged her eighty-six-year-old husband to have a baby with her maid Hagar, instead. Hagar and Abram had a son called Ishmael, but rather than cheering Sarai up, it saddened her.

Abram turned ninety-nine years old and Sarai reached ninety, and still they had no

child of their own. However God insisted
that His promise remained true. "I want
you and your wife to change your names as
a sign of my vow," He said. "From now on,
you will not be Abram and Sarai, but
Abraham and Sarah. Do what I say and
trust me, and everything I have told you
will come true. You and Sarah will have
your own baby next year, you'll see. I want
you to call him Isaac."

So Abraham and Sarah continued to
wait.

Genesis chapters 11 to 13, 15 to 17

God's Promise Comes True

At long last, when Abraham was one hundred years old, Sarah had a baby boy whom they called Isaac. Everything had come to pass just as God had said.

The couple were so overjoyed that they thought nothing could spoil their happiness. But gradually, Sarah became eaten up with

envy of Abraham's other son, Ishmael,
whom he had with Sarah's maid, Hagar.
There had been trouble between the two
women ever since Hagar had become
pregnant. Because she was carrying
Abraham's baby, Hagar had put on airs
and graces and looked down on her
mistress. Sarah had become so
annoyed that she had treated Hagar
badly. So badly that Hagar had
eventually run away. An
angel found Hagar weeping
by a desert spring and
comforted her, convincing her
to return. God reassured Sarah
too. He said that He would make Abraham
and Hagar's son, Ishmael, the founder of a

53

great race. But when Abraham and Sarah had a son, Isaac, it would be his descendants who would be God's own special people.

However when Isaac was born, the rivalry Sarah felt toward Hagar brewed again. Ishmael was about fourteen and he was fond of his little brother, but Sarah hated seeing them together. She couldn't stand to be reminded that because both boys had the same father, her maid's son was equally important.

"Get rid of them!" Sarah begged Abraham. "I don't want Ishmael around, taking what should rightfully be Isaac's."

Abraham was upset because he loved both his sons. He asked God what to do.

"Don't worry," God reassured him. "Do as Sarah suggests. I'll look after Hagar and Ishmael. Trust me."

Next morning, Abraham told Hagar that she and Ishmael had to leave. With a heavy heart, he gave them food and a waterskin, and turned them out into the desert.

God kept His word and looked after Abraham's first son and his mother as they struggled to survive on their own. Once, when they were close to dying of thirst, God sent an angel to them with water. God stayed at Ishmael's side as he grew up, and he became strong and brave. Just as God had promised, He made Ishmael the founder of a great nation—the Arabs.

Genesis chapters 16, 17

A Terrible Test
for Abraham

God had put Abraham through two very difficult tests—having to journey into the unknown and having to wait for so long for he and Sarah to have a child. But the hardest test was yet to come. When their beloved son Isaac was about eleven years old, God delivered Abraham some shattering news.

"I want you to take your son to Moriah, to a place that I will show you," God told Abraham, "and offer me a sacrifice. I don't want you to kill and burn a goat or a lamb as usual, I want you to sacrifice Isaac." Abraham was appalled. But God had spoken clearly and Abraham was quite sure what He wanted. Next morning, with agony in his heart, Abraham organized two servants to make ready to go, with firewood and provisions packed onto a donkey. Abraham told Isaac they were going on a trip, and they set off into the desert.

For two days, Abraham walked closer to the place where he was to perform the terrible deed. Then, on the third day of traveling, they came to the foot of a hill and Abraham knew it was the place God meant. "You stay here with the donkey," Abraham told the servants. "I'm going up the hill with Isaac to pray and make an offering to God."

Isaac hurried to help, unloading the donkey and lifting up the heavy bundle of wood they would need to burn the sacrifice. Abraham carried a sharp knife and a pot of red-hot coals for starting the fire.

Then the old man and his son began climbing, higher and higher, until they could no longer see the servants waiting below. At last they came to a little clearing and Abraham stopped and said in a strange, tense voice, "Here's the spot."

"Father, we've got the wood and coals to light the fire, but we've forgotten to bring an animal to sacrifice," pointed out Isaac.

Abraham couldn't bring himself to meet his son's eyes. "God will give us the animal," he said, his voice cracking with sorrow.

Then the two worked side by side to make an altar from stones and they arranged the firewood on top of it. Finally, the time had come for Abraham to do the unthinkable.

Imagine Isaac's terror when his father tied him up and lifted him onto the wood, realizing that HE was to be the sacrifice.

In anguish, Abraham raised his knife high and took a deep breath, steeling himself to kill his own son, whom he loved so much.

Just as he was about to plunge the blade downward— "STOP!" boomed a voice from Heaven into Abraham's mind. Abraham knew it was an angel speaking. "You have proved that you love God perfectly by showing you were ready to sacrifice your son, just because He said so. That is enough—do not harm Isaac."

Abraham dropped the knife. His shaking hands could hardly untie the rope that bound Isaac. Weeping so hard he thought his chest would burst, he held his beloved son, and asked for his forgiveness.

Through his tears, Abraham caught sight of a nearby bush shaking—a ram was caught in it. "You see, Isaac. I told you that God would give us an animal for the sacrifice!" Abraham went over and caught the ram and offered it in Isaac's place.

When Abraham and his son had finished praying, they walked down the hill and returned home together.

Genesis chapter 22

A Tale of
Twin Brothers

Isaac's mother, Sarah, lived to be one hundred and twenty-seven years old, while his father, Abraham, lived to one hundred and seventy-five. By the time they both died, Isaac had married a girl called Rebecca, from Abraham's old town of Haran. Isaac inherited his father's farming business and stayed in Canaan, following God's will just as Abraham had done.

Like Isaac's father and mother, he and Rebecca had to wait a long time before God sent them children—twenty years. It was worth the wait, for when Rebecca finally found herself expecting a baby it was not one, but two—twins! A short time before they were born, God told Rebecca, "You are having two sons, who will lead two peoples. One boy will be stronger than the other and the older one will serve the younger one." At the birth, a very strange thing happened. The second baby came out holding the first one's heel, as though he wanted to pull his older brother back and overtake. Isaac and Rebecca called the elder boy Esau, because the name means "hairy" and Esau was dark and had lots of hair. They named their younger son Jacob, which means "someone who wants to seize somebody else's place."

Time passed and the twins grew very different in personality as well as looks. Jacob was quiet and thoughtful. He loved spending time at home with his mother in the kitchen, and they became very close. However, Esau was strong and brave. He loved roaming around outside and he became an excellent hunter. Esau was his father's favorite son.

Whenever Jacob saw his father and brother together, talking and laughing in easy companionship, he couldn't help but wish that he was loved best by Isaac instead. To make matters worse, because Esau had been born before Jacob, the law said that Esau was to be given all of their father's wealth when he died. This was called his birthright. Jacob knew that he was cleverer than Esau and better suited to running his father's business. He couldn't stand to think that it was Esau's birthright to take it over eventually.

One day, Jacob was cooking a delicious bean stew when Esau arrived back from a hunt. "Ooooh, what's that? I'm

STARVING!" he exclaimed, bending over the cooking pot and breathing in the aroma. "Can I have some now?" he begged.

Jacob's eyes glinted with a sudden idea. "I'll give you some stew," he replied, "if you promise to give me all your rights as the firstborn son."

"Done!" agreed Esau. All he could think about was his rumbling stomach, burning with hunger. "If I don't get anything to eat within the next five minutes I'll fall over and die anyway, so what use would my birthright be then?" he joked.

But Jacob was quite serious. "Say you solemnly swear," he insisted.

"I solemnly swear," promised Esau. "Now come on, give me that stew!"

Jacob ladled some stew into a bowl and gave Esau some soft, baked bread, and both twins sat back, highly pleased.

Twenty years passed and Isaac was an old, blind man who knew he didn't have long to live. One of Isaac's last wishes was for Esau to go hunting for meat for his favorite meal. Afterward, Isaac was going to give his eldest son the blessing that officially gave him his birthright. Esau gladly set off with his bow and arrows at once.

But Rebecca had overheard. All at once, a plan came to her to trick her husband into giving her favorite son Jacob the blessing instead! First, she quickly cooked the meal her husband had asked for. Then she hurriedly dressed Jacob in Esau's clothes, so he would smell like his brother, and wrapped goatskin round his arms and neck so he would feel hairy like his brother too.

"But– But– " protested Jacob.

"I'll take the blame," Rebecca reassured her son, and sent him in with the food to see his father.

The trick worked perfectly. Isaac was at first suspicious because his tasty dinner had arrived so quickly, but Jacob said that God had helped him in his hunting. Jacob copied

Esau's voice and, of course, he smelled and felt like his brother too. Isaac was fooled into thinking that Jacob was Esau, and gave him the all-important birthright blessing.

When Esau arrived back from the hunt and went to his father, they both quickly realized they had been tricked. How they wept with frustration and regret. However it was too late, the old man could not take back his blessing.

Later, in private, Esau began to feel angry. "I'll wait until father dies," he swore to himself, "but no longer than that. Then I shall have my revenge on Jacob."

Genesis chapters 25 to 28

Jacob's Dream

Jacob had won his twin brother Esau's birthright, but his joy soon melted into shame and regret. His old, blind father was so bitterly disappointed that he could hardly talk to Jacob, and Esau couldn't stand the sight of him either. It was only because Esau didn't want to upset his father even further that he hadn't already taken revenge on his smaller, weaker twin brother. Only Jacob's mother still loved him—and now he was about to lose her too. Rebecca was so worried about what Esau would do to her favorite son once Isaac died, that she told Jacob he had no choice but to leave. "You must go far away, well out of Esau's reach," Rebecca urged. "Hurry to my brother, your Uncle Laban, in the city of Haran. You'll be safe there. We'll just have to hope that your brother cools down and forgives you, so you can come back."

So Jacob left his home and his family in disgrace, with no one for company and no possessions for comfort. He set off for Haran through the desert, wondering why he had

done what he had done. At the end of the
first lonely day's traveling, Jacob came
across a rocky, sheltered spot where he
could camp for the night. Weary and
miserable, Jacob found a flattish, smooth
stone that would have to do as a pillow
and laid down to try to get some rest.

Alone in the desert, hungry, cold, and
worried about wild animals, Jacob did
not sleep well. He tossed and turned for
hours, and when he did eventually fall
asleep he had a very strange dream.

Jacob dreamed that a blinding light
suddenly burst from the dark night sky. He
shielded his eyes and blinked until he got
used to the glare and could open them
properly. Then Jacob saw that the light

shone in a steady, sloping beam
down to the ground. People in
bright, shimmering clothes were
gliding up and down. With a
shock, Jacob realized that he was
looking at a staircase from Heaven
to Earth and that the people were
angels. Suddenly he felt God
Himself standing beside him.

"Yes, I am the Lord," said God.
"And as I promised your
grandfather Abraham
and your father Isaac, I
am going to give the
land on which
you are
lying to

you and your family. You will have as many descendants as there are specks of dust on the ground. Now remember, you will never be alone. I will always be with you. I will look after you, and wherever you go, I will make sure that one day you return safely back home."

Then the staircase and the angels faded away and the voice was gone. Jacob woke up, lying stiff and cold on his own in the desert. But he knew God had been there and was watching over him.

Genesis chapters 27, 28

Joseph the Dreamer

Jacob was one of the wealthiest men in Canaan. He had vast herds of cattle, sheep, goats, camels, and donkeys, and he owned many tents, filled with possessions. However the thing he held most dear was Joseph, his eleventh son. Joseph's mother was Jacob's true love, Rachel. The couple had

waited for many years before God sent
them a child. So long that Jacob had
ten sons by three other wives by then.
So Joseph was very special.

Unfortunately, Jacob made it
obvious that Joseph was his favorite.
He sometimes kept Joseph at home
with him while his other sons
went into the fields on
farming duties. Of course
this made Jacob's other sons
resentful of their brother.
Even more so when
Joseph turned
seventeen. Jacob
had an expensive
coat made for him. It was a

beautiful, long coat with big sleeves, richly sewn with many different colors. It drove Jacob's other sons wild with jealousy.

The situation went from bad to worse when Joseph began to have strange dreams.

"Guess what?" he asked his brothers one morning. "Last night, I dreamed that we were in the fields at harvest time tying the wheat into sheaves, when my sheaf stood up straight. Then your sheaves gathered around it and bowed to mine!"

"Who do you think you are?" spat one of the brothers.

"Do you see yourself as better than us?" growled another.

"Do you think you're going to be a king and rule over us?" scowled a third.

A little while later, Joseph had another odd dream and again made the mistake of telling his brothers about it.

"I dreamed last night that I saw the sun, the moon, and eleven stars all bowing down to me." The brothers knew that Joseph meant that their father, mother, and the eleven of them were like his servants. How furious they were!

One day, when Jacob had kept Joseph at home with him and sent his other sons out to work, he decided to send Joseph to check on them. Out in the hot fields, the tired, thirsty brothers saw him coming, fresh from home, all dressed up in his fancy coat and they had a terrible idea.

"Here comes the dreamer!" one of them

laughed. "I wish we could get rid of him once and for all."

"Well, this is our chance," another said.

"There's no one around, it's the perfect opportunity!" a third brother agreed.

"Let's kill him and throw the body into that pit over there," another brother urged.

"We could tell our father that he was attacked by wild animals!" one suggested.

"Stop!" cried the eldest brother, Reuben, horrified. "We can't kill Joseph! Do you really want his blood on your hands? If you must, throw him into that old, dry well over there and leave him—but don't murder him!" (Little did the brothers know that once they'd all gone home, Reuben intended to sneak back and rescue Joseph).

And that's what the brothers did. They fell on Joseph, ripping off his special coat, and then lowered him into the dried-up well, taking away the rope.

Pleased, the brothers ignored Joseph's cries for help, and sat down to eat—all except Reuben. He stomped off to see to the animals in the furthest pastures.

While Reuben was gone, a camel train of spice traders passed by on their way to Egypt. One of the brothers, Judah, had another awful idea. "Reuben was right. We shouldn't harm Joseph—he is our flesh and blood, after all," he announced, with a glint in his eye. "I have a better plan—we'll sell him instead. I'm sure the traders will pay a good price for a slave."

By the time Reuben returned, Judah and the brothers had accepted twenty pieces of silver from the traders and Joseph was gone.

"What have you done?" Reuben cried. "Shame on you, Judah. Shame on you all! Now what are you going to tell Father?"

In desperation, the brothers came up with a final part to their wicked plan. They killed a young goat, dipped Joseph's torn coat in its blood, and took it home to show their father. "Joseph was killed and eaten by wild animals," they explained to Jacob.

The old man collapsed in sorrow, weeping and mourning for his beloved Joseph. "I will grieve for my son until the day I die," he sobbed.

Genesis chapter 37

A Slave
in Egypt

Sold by his family, marched by strangers all the way to a foreign land, and then traded in the market place as a slave— Joseph was exhausted and terrified. Yet his strong character must have shone through because the man who bought Joseph trusted him to work in his house, not in his fields or as a laborer. The man was very important and wealthy. His name was Potiphar and he was captain of the soldiers who guarded Pharaoh, the king of Egypt. God stayed with Joseph all the time and cheered him up, helping him do his duties well. Potiphar was so pleased that he kept promoting Joseph. After a while, Joseph was running Potiphar's whole household.

Now Joseph was not only hardworking and trustworthy, he was also quite handsome. So much so that Potiphar's wife fell in love with him. Each day, she seized every opportunity behind her husband's back to flirt with Joseph, trying to tempt him into having an affair. Joseph was loyal to Potiphar and kept turning her down. But

Potiphar's wife was determined to get what she wanted. One day, she lay in wait for Joseph and grabbed him by his cloak. Joseph had to wriggle out of it in order to escape her clutches and run off! Then the scorned woman saw a way to get her own back. She put on a show of being deeply upset and accused Joseph of having forced his way into her bedroom. She said that when she screamed out, he had ran away, leaving only his cloak behind.

Of course, Potiphar was furious. He had Joseph flung into prison.

Joseph could have wept and wailed. He could have despaired and died, but God stayed with him and lifted his spirits. The jailer was fond of the reliable, capable young man and began giving him special jobs. Soon, he put Joseph in charge of all the other prisoners.

Two of the prisoners in Joseph's care were Pharaoh's butler and baker. One morning, Joseph found them looking anxious because they had both had strange dreams that they couldn't understand.

"Tell me about them," Joseph urged. "Maybe God will explain to me what they're about."

"I dreamed I saw a vine on which three branches of grapes grew," said the butler. "I picked them and squeezed them into Pharaoh's cup and gave him the juice to drink."

Joseph felt sure he knew what the dream meant, thanks to God. "In three days' time Pharaoh is going to pardon you and give you your job back," he explained.

The butler was delighted. "Oh thank you! Thank you so much!" he cried.

"My friend," Joseph said, "just promise me that when you're released, you won't forget about me. Please tell Pharaoh about me and beg him to release me, for I don't deserve to be in here!"

"Well, what about my dream?" asked

the baker excitedly. "I dreamed I was carrying three baskets of white bread on my head, and the birds were eating the bread out of the top basket."

Joseph's face fell as the meaning came to him. "I hate to tell you this," he said sadly, "but in three days' time, Pharaoh is going to hang you."

The dreams came true. In three days' time, the baker was put to death, while the butler was released and set back to work for Pharaoh. He was so joyful that any thoughts of Joseph went out of his head. Joseph remained in prison, quite forgotten.

Genesis chapters 39, 40

The Ruler
of Egypt

One morning, there was a commotion in the royal palace of Egypt. Pharaoh had awoken deeply troubled. He had had two strange dreams, which he was sure meant something but he had no idea what. In the first dream, Pharaoh had been standing by the River Nile. Seven fat cows

came out of
the waters and
started grazing. Then
came seven more
cows—but this time all
skin and bones. The thin
cows ate up the fat cows, but
they didn't look any healthier. In the
second dream, Pharaoh saw seven ears
of corn growing on a stalk. They ripened
and turned golden. Then he noticed seven
small, shriveled ears of corn sprouting and
they swallowed up the big, full ears.

Pharaoh had summoned all his wise
men, but none of them had an explanation.
Suddenly, the butler remembered Joseph.

Two years had passed and he wasn't even sure if Joseph was still alive. But now he told Pharaoh all about the amazing young Israelite man locked in the dungeon.

Pharaoh sent for him at once. Joseph was hauled out of prison and brought into the magnificent courtroom of the great King of Egypt. Then Pharaoh described his dreams and Joseph felt God give him the interpretation.

"Both dreams mean the same," Joseph announced to the anxiously waiting king. "For the next seven years, Egypt will have excellent harvests. But during the following seven years the crops will fail and there will be a terrible famine. Here's what God says to do. Hire a minister with officials under him to take charge of your kingdom. For the next seven years, they should collect one fifth of all the grain that is grown and store it away in warehouses. During the seven years of famine, you can share out the grain so your people don't starve."

"Really?" said Pharaoh. "Is that what your God thinks?" He thought for a while and everyone in the courtroom held their breath to see whether the king was pleased.

Pharaoh descended from his gleaming throne and approached Joseph. He took a huge gold ring off his finger and gave it to the former prisoner. "You will be the minister," he ordered. "I can't think of anyone better. You start straight away."

Genesis chapter 41

The Silver Cup

Joseph was now thirty years old, and Pharaoh's right-hand man. He had more power in Egypt than anyone, except the king himself.

Seven years passed. Then, as predicted, the crops failed, and not just in Egypt but in all the countries nearby. Fortunately,

Joseph had made sure that the Egyptian warehouses were fully stocked. And as news of the stores spread, starving people came from far and wide to ask for food.

Among them were Joseph's brothers from Canaan. Joseph's father, Jacob, only sent ten of his sons to Egypt to buy grain. After losing Joseph he couldn't bear to part with his and Rachel's only other son, Benjamin, so he had kept him at home.

More than twenty years had passed since the brothers had sold Joseph into slavery. Joseph was now married to an Egyptian. He acted like an Egyptian. He looked like a magnificent Egyptian prince. He even spoke Egyptian. So of course, when the brothers were called into his

presence to buy grain, they didn't recognize him, but Joseph knew who they were. He was disappointed that Benjamin—his favorite brother—wasn't with them, so Joseph decided to trick them in order to get to see him.

"I don't believe you have come to ask for grain," Joseph told his brothers through an interpreter. "I think you are spies!"

"We're not spies, we're brothers!" they protested. "We were twelve, but one died long ago and the youngest of us is at home with our father."

"Then prove it," Joseph ordered. "One of you must journey back and fetch your youngest brother. I'll give you some time to think about who is going to go." And he had them all thrown in prison.

After three days, Joseph ordered the brothers to be brought in front of him again.

"I've decided to let you return home with the grain you need," he announced. "But you must still bring me your youngest brother and to make sure you do, I shall keep one of you here as hostage."

He clapped his hands and at once, his servants grabbed Simeon, tying him up and taking him away.

It was with heavy hearts that the nine brothers set off to Canaan. They were even more dismayed when they discovered that the money they had paid for the grain was somehow in their sacks. "What's happened?" they wondered, "This is going to land us in deeper trouble." They had no idea that Joseph had ordered his servants to put the money there as another trick.

When they told Jacob that they had to return to Egypt with Benjamin, the anguished old man cried, "No! No way! I've lost Joseph, and now Simeon has gone. I'm not letting Benjamin out of my sight!"

But the weeks went by and the famine grew worse and eventually the Egyptian corn was used up. Jacob had no choice but to send his sons back to buy more—this time with Benjamin. The grief-stricken old man loaded them down with expensive gifts for the powerful Egyptian minister in the hope that he would be pleased and allow all ten of his sons to return.

As soon as Joseph heard that his brothers had arrived back in Egypt, he ordered them to be brought to the palace. The men were terrified they were going to be arrested for taking the money they had found in their sacks. "It was a mistake," they told Joseph's steward, giving it back. "Look—it's all here, count it."

But Joseph hadn't invited them to his house for that. Instead, he gave them a feast. Joseph was so delighted to see Benjamin that he gave him five times as much to eat and drink as the others!

Next day, all ten brothers were hugely relieved to find that they were allowed to set off back to Canaan with all the grain they could carry.

However, they hadn't gone far when they heard pounding hooves behind them, and when they looked it was Joseph's steward chasing after them. He insisted on opening the brothers' sacks, from eldest to youngest, and in the last one, Benjamin's, was Joseph's best silver cup!

"Thieves!" accused the steward,

knowing it was another of Joseph's tricks.

In utter despair, the brothers went with the steward back to the city and begged Joseph for forgiveness.

"Your punishment will be that Benjamin must stay here and be my slave," Joseph announced. "The rest of you are free to go."

Then Judah sprang up and pleaded, "Your Highness, our father has already lost his favorite son. If we return without this boy, he will surely die of grief. I beg you—let me stay and be your slave instead."

Then Joseph felt that his heart would break. "Everybody out!" he ordered, and his advisors left him alone with his brothers. Finally he told them who he was. "Don't blame yourselves for selling me into slavery," Joseph told the astonished men with great grace. "It was all part of God's plan for me." Then he threw his arms around Benjamin in tears, and hugged and kissed them all.

Pharaoh was delighted when he heard that Joseph had a family who were alive and well. He invited them all to live in one of the lushest parts of Egypt, where Joseph could look after them.

Jacob was reunited with his beloved son, Joseph, and lived out the last few years of his life in happiness.

Genesis chapters 41 to 46

The Baby in
the Basket

Joseph and his brothers lived in Egypt for the rest of their lives and had many children, grandchildren, and great-grandchildren. They did well in farming and business and became wealthy and powerful. As time passed, the Egyptians began calling them Israelites after the special name God had given to Jacob. Years went by and the number of Israelites grew, and different pharaohs came and went. After four hundred years, one king became particularly worried because there were so many Israelites. He told his advisors, "I am worried that if there was ever a war, the Israelites might turn against us and join with our enemies to defeat Egypt. We must find a way to stop their numbers growing further and to make them less powerful."

Pharaoh decided on drastic action—he sent his soldiers to seize the Israelites and turn them into slaves. Then he appointed slave-drivers to set the Israelites to work, laboring on roads and building sites, and in the fields.

But still the number of Israelites increased, and families spread further throughout Egypt. Furious, Pharaoh came up with an even more wicked plan. He ordered his soldiers to search out every newborn Israelite boy and kill them all!

Of course, many desperate families tried to hide their beloved babies. One woman, who already had a daughter, Miriam, and a son, Aaron, kept her newborn boy hidden for three months. But as time went on, he became bigger and noisier and harder to conceal. In the end, the desperate woman took a reed basket and covered it with tar so it was watertight. She gently laid her baby in it and took it down to the River Nile, setting it in the thick, tall grasses at the water's edge so it wouldn't float away. She told Miriam to stay a little way off to see that the baby was alright.

It wasn't long before the little girl saw a grand procession making its way down to the river. Her eyes opened wide at the sight of a young woman in magnificent robes, splendid jewels, and rich makeup, accompanied by many servants and slaves. It was the princess, coming to bathe! The little girl watched, hardly daring to breathe, as the princess caught sight of the basket in the rushes and sent a servant to bring it to her. As soon as the princess saw the baby boy inside, she realized that he must be an Israelite. As she lifted the baby up, he began to cry and her heart melted with pity for

the hungry, helpless child. She decided to take the baby home and keep him.

Bravely, Miriam dared to approach the princess, curtseying low. "Would you like me to find an Israelite nurse to look after him, Your Highness?" she suggested nervously.

The princess was pleased, and the little girl dashed home and fetched her mother!

So the little boy was at first cared for by his real mother, then given the education of an Egyptian prince. For the princess loved him so much, she adopted him as her own son. She called him Moses, which means "to draw out," because she had rescued him by having him drawn out of the water.

Exodus chapters 1, 2

The Burning Bush

Moses was brought up as Egyptian royalty, but he knew that he was an Israelite by birth. As he grew up, he found it unbearable that he was living a rich, comfortable life of freedom, while other Israelites suffered as Egyptian slaves. One day, when he was a young man, he saw an

Egyptian guard savagely hitting an Israelite man, and something inside him snapped. Moses beat the guard off, leaving him lying dead at his feet. News of his crime quickly spread. Moses knew that even the princess would not be able to save him from a terrible punishment, perhaps even death. He had no choice but to run away.

Moses fled to a country called Midian and settled into the quiet life of a shepherd. He looked after the flocks belonging to a village priest named Jethro, and he married his daughter, Zipporah. Years came and went and Moses' former life as an Egyptian royal seemed like a dream.

One day, Moses was out with his sheep when he came upon a very strange sight.

A bush was on fire, but the leaves
and branches of the bush
weren't burning away.
While Moses marveled, a
voice suddenly boomed,
"Moses, come no
closer to this holy
place! I am God—
the God of your
fathers, Abraham,
Isaac, and Jacob."

Moses fell to
the ground, covering his
face in terror.

"I have seen how my people,
the Israelites, suffer in Egypt," echoed the
voice. "But I will free them from slavery

and return them to Canaan, a land of plenty that I promised would be their own. I want you to return to Egypt and rescue my people. Convince them to follow you and demand Pharaoh to release them."

Moses was shocked. "No one will believe that my orders are from you, Lord," he protested.

God gave Moses three special signs so that he could prove it. Firstly, if Moses threw his shepherd's staff onto the ground, it turned into a snake! As soon as he picked it up again, it turned back into wood. Secondly, if Moses thrust his hand into his robe, it came out covered with scales and sores of the disease leprosy! When he put it back again, it was healed and healthy.

Lastly, God told Moses that if he poured some water from the River Nile onto the ground, it would turn into blood!

Moses was stunned, but even so, he was still unsure. "How can I be a leader, Lord?" he argued. "I don't even like talking in public. I go red and can't get the words out. Isn't there someone else you can send?"

"I have already told your brother Aaron to come and find you—he can do the talking," insisted God.

Moses hurried home and explained to his wife and his father-in-law what he had been ordered to do. To Moses' great surprise, Jethro believed him. God reassured Moses that it was safe for him to return to Egypt as a new pharaoh had come to the throne.

So he and his wife packed up and set off through the countryside.

As they neared Egypt, Aaron came out to meet them, just as God had promised. The long-lost brothers hurried to see the Israelite elders straight away. While Aaron explained that God had told Moses to lead the Israelites out of slavery, Moses proved that his message was from God by demonstrating the three magic signs in front of everyone. How the Israelites gasped! They believed Moses and sent up prayers of thanks that God had sent them help.

Exodus chapters 2 to 4

The Nine
Plagues of Egypt

As God had ordered, Moses and Aaron requested an audience with Pharaoh himself. They were summoned to appear in Pharaoh's magnificent courtroom, in front of all his guards, advisors, and magicians. "We have come at God's command to ask that you set the people of Israel free!" the brothers dared to tell Pharaoh.

But Pharaoh just laughed and waved for Moses and Aaron to be taken away. Then he set the Israelites even tougher tasks to do, making their lives even harder and more miserable.

"I've made the situation worse!" Moses told God, but God insisted that he try again.

So once more Moses and Aaron went to see Pharaoh. This time Aaron threw down Moses' staff, which turned into a snake, wriggling on the floor. Pharaoh signaled to his magicians and they too threw their staffs onto the floor, which also turned

into slithering snakes. Pharaoh didn't even care when Aaron's snake swallowed up all of the magicians' snakes. "Audience over," he announced coldly.

Moses despaired, but God told him what to do. Early the next day, Moses and Aaron went down to the River Nile and waited for Pharaoh to take his morning walk there. When Pharaoh refused their demands, Aaron hit the waters with the staff. At once, the Nile turned to blood. The river ran red for seven days—all the fish died and there was no water to drink.

Yet the cold-hearted king was unmoved. Then Moses signaled Aaron to stretch the

staff over the Nile, and millions of frogs
came hopping out of every river, stream,
and pond in Egypt. Everywhere anyone
looked there were frogs… anything
anyone touched had frogs on it… the
people couldn't move for frogs!

Then Pharaoh sent for Moses. "Tell your
god to make this stop and I will let your
people go."

Immediately, there were so many
dead frogs that the Egyptians had to pile
them into huge, stinking heaps.

Pharaoh went back on his word.

So God ordered Moses to tell Aaron
to hit the ground with the staff. The dust
swirled and billions of lice swarmed out
of the ground and over Egypt. Soon,

everything that had been slimy with leaping frogs was itching with biting lice.

But Pharaoh's heart was as hard as stone.

So God sent vast clouds of flies humming into Egypt. They darkened the skies and blanketed the ground, dive bombing people's heads, landing on their eyelids, fluttering up their nostrils. But not one fly entered the house of an Israelite.

Then Pharaoh summoned Moses. "I will do as you ask," he announced, "if your god rids us of these flies!"

Once again, as soon as the flies were gone, Pharaoh simply broke his promise.

So God sent a dreadful disease which wiped out every horse, camel, ox, goat, and sheep in the land—except for those belonging to the Israelites.

Still, Pharaoh would not give in.

Then God told Moses and Aaron to take
a handful of ashes and throw it up into the
air. As the wind blew the ashes across Egypt,
an awful sickness spread, which caused
terrible boils to break out over every person
and each remaining animal—unless they
were Israelite.

It just made Pharaoh more determined.

So God told Moses to stretch his staff up
to the heavens… Thunder crashed, lighting
flashed, and hail fell from the skies in
mighty torrents, flattening trees and plants.
Everywhere except in the fields belonging
to the Israelites.

At last Pharaoh called Moses again.

"Enough!" he spat. "Make it stop and I will do what you ask." Moses prayed and the storm calmed. "I lied," announced Pharaoh triumphantly. He turned on his heel and strode away.

The very next day, a strange wind blew across Egypt, thick with locusts. Within a few hours they had eaten every blade of grass, every leaf, every ear of corn, every fruit on the trees.

"Aaaaaaargh!" howled Pharaoh. "Alright, the Israelites can go." The wind changed direction and the locusts were blown into the Red Sea and drowned.

But still, Pharaoh did not go through with his promise. So God told Moses to stretch out his hand and Egypt was swamped in total darkness for three days and nights. As his miserable people stumbled around blindly and the country ground to a halt, Pharaoh once again summoned Moses. "The Israelites may go, and this time I will not go back on my word," he spat, his eyes full of hate. "As long as they leave all their sheep, goats, camels, and donkeys."

Moses listened to God.

"No," he replied, and Pharaoh turned white with fury.

"Then get out," roared the cruel king. "Your people will be my slaves forever. If I ever lay eyes on you again, you will die!"

Exodus chapters 5 to 10

121

The First Passover

God spoke to Moses and said, "I am going to send one last plague upon Egypt, so terrible that Pharaoh will be glad to let the Israelites go. At midnight, every firstborn child in Egypt shall die. From the firstborn of Pharaoh to the firstborn of the lowliest servant to the firstborn of every

animal. No one shall escape—unless they
are an Israelite. Here's what they have to do
to be spared. Every family must cook a
lamb and smear their doorposts with the
blood. Then I shall know which houses are
Israelite homes. Forever after, this day will
be called Passover and celebrated as the first
day of the year. By my passing over the
land tonight, my people will be set free—
the beginning of a new era."

Next morning, nothing could be heard in
Egypt except for wailing and screaming as
people discovered their loved ones were
dead. People and animals had breathed
their last in every household across the
land—except for the homes of the Israelites.

Once again Moses and Aaron found

themselves before Pharaoh, who was weeping over his own dead firstborn son. "Take your people and go!" he whispered. "Be gone, and never darken my lands again."

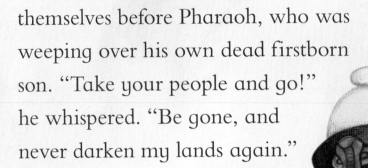

All over Pharaoh's country, the doomed Egyptians were so desperate to be rid of the Israelites that they offered them gold, silver, and jewels to leave right away.

And that is how over six hundred thousand men, women, and children came to walk out of Egypt. After more than four hundred years of captivity, the Israelites were heading home.

Exodus chapters 11, 12

Escape Across the Red Sea

God Himself guided the Israelites as they traveled out of Egypt and into the wilderness beyond. By day He appeared as a column of cloud and by night, as a column of fire, so they could follow Him.

The Israelites had reached the sands of the Red Sea when they noticed a massive cloud of dust behind them in the distance, rushing toward them at great speed.

It was the Egyptian army! The minute that Pharaoh had ordered the Israelites to leave, he regretted his decision. In a whirlwind of hatred, he called for his best armor and ordered six hundred of his finest charioteers to make ready to chase after his former slaves.

The Israelites were terrified and turned on Moses. "Did you lead us out of captivity only to meet our deaths in the desert?" they cried.

"Don't be afraid," Moses told the Israelites. "The Lord will protect you, wait and see." And God spoke to Moses, telling him what to do.

With the Egyptian army thundering ever closer, Moses urged the Israelites forward— straight toward the Red Sea. Then the column of cloud blew over Pharaoh and his charioteers, smothering them so they couldn't see their way ahead. While the bewildered, frustrated Egyptians were forced to slow their pace, Moses reached the foaming seashore and stretched out his hand toward the ocean.

An immense wind blew up, nearly sweeping the Israelites off their feet. It howled and hurled, and with great gusts this way and that it split the waves. The wind drove the waters to the right and left, higher and higher, until they rolled back leaving a wide pathway of seabed in between. Then bravely and boldly, Moses strode down the sand, leading the Israelites between the towering walls of water on either side.

Then came the Egyptian army, galloping forward. How petrified they were when they saw the waters of the Red Sea divided in front of them. Yet they plunged into the passage as the last of the Israelites reached the sandy shore on the other side.

As Pharaoh and his charioteers sped ever closer to the Israelites, Moses stretched out his hand once more. Then the towering walls of water teetered, toppled, and crashed down. The Red Sea closed over the Egyptians, drowning each and every one, and the Israelites were truly free at last.

Exodus chapters 13, 14

The Ten Commandments

After three months of wandering through the hot, rocky desert, the Israelites arrived at the foot of the holy mountain of Sinai. Moses announced they would camp there a while. He told them that they should make ready with prayers and rituals because in three days' time God was going to speak to all of them.

Sure enough, on the morning of the third day, black storm clouds gathered around the peak of the mountain, hiding it from view. Thunder rumbled and lightning split the skies. Then the earth shook, and the mountain began to spew out flames and smoke as if it were an enormous furnace. A sound like a giant trumpet blared out through the air, calling the terrified Israelites to assemble at the foot of the mountain. Then Moses slowly climbed up and up toward the smoking, fiery mountaintop and disappeared from view into the clouds.

For a long time after he had gone, thunder continued to echo around the

slopes and many Israelites thought it was
the voice of God talking to their leader.
When the noise had at last died away,
Moses came back down the mountain and
announced that God had given him ten
important rules of behavior:

1. *You must not worship any other god but me.*

2. *You must not make a statue or a picture to worship.*

3. *You must only use my name respectfully.*

4. *You must keep the seventh day, or Sabbath, of every
    week as a holy day of rest.*

5. *You must always be respectful to your parents.*

6. *You must never commit murder.*

7. *You must never be unfaithful to your partner.*

8. *You must not steal.*

9. *You must not lie.*

10. *You must not envy the things that other people have.*

Moses wrote the Ten Commandments down, and lots of other rules too. The very next day he built an altar at the foot of the mountain and asked the Israelites to vow to obey the rules. Then Moses made a sacrifice to seal their solemn promise.

Yet God still had more that He wanted the Israelites to learn, so He summoned Moses up the mountain once more, where they could talk on their own together. The Israelites watched as their leader climbed up the mountain one more time and disappeared alone into the dark clouds.

The Israelites watched and waited for Moses to return… watched and waited for seven long weeks, but there was no sign of their leader. Worried and confused, they came to the conclusion that God had abandoned them and Moses would never return.

"Make something for us to worship," they begged Aaron. "We need something we can see and touch." Thousands of men and women brought Aaron their gold jewelry. He melted it down and made an enormous statue of a calf, one of the animals that was sometimes sacrificed to God. To please the people and keep them under control, Aaron even built the calf an enormous altar and declared there would be a festival in its honor.

The people were delighted. At last they had a straightforward god. One that wasn't invisible and didn't speak to them in thunder, giving them complicated lists of things they should and shouldn't do. Immediately, the Israelites began praying to the calf and offering it sacrifices, and singing and dancing around it.

As they did so, Moses came clambering down the mountainside at last. He held two huge stone tablets on which God Himself had written out the ten most important commandments so that no one could forget them or get them wrong.

Moses knew already about how the Israelites were worshiping the golden calf because God had told him while they were

up the mountain. God had been full of fury
and so was Moses. Enraged at the sight that
met his eyes as he approached the
camp, he flung the stone tablets to
the ground and they shattered into
pieces. Then he hurled the golden
calf into the flames of one of the
sacrificial fires. "Aaron, what did
everyone do to you that you
allowed this to happen?" Moses
was disgusted at his
brother. Then he
called for anyone
who was on
God's side to go and
stand next to him. Only the men of the
tribe of Levi took up places next to Moses.

On God's orders, he told each of them to grab a sword and put to death everyone who stood in their way as punishment for their sins.

Over three thousand Israelites were killed that night. The next day, Moses went back up the mountain to pray to God for forgiveness for the wickedness of His Chosen People.

Exodus chapters 19 to 24, 32

Joshua and the Battle of Jericho

The Israelites had to fight against the tribes in the lands around Canaan for many years. So many that Moses never got to enter the country that God had chosen for his people. When the time drew near that Moses realized he was going to die, he climbed up to a mountaintop and

God showed him the Promised Land
spread out far below. And so Moses died
comforted, and a warrior called Joshua
took over as ruler of the Israelites.

Then God told Joshua to be brave and
bold. It was finally time to cross the River
Jordan, which was all that remained to
keep the Israelites from entering the
Promised Land. So Joshua told the people
to prepare to fight. Meanwhile, he sent
spies across the river into the city of
Jericho to find out what they were up
against. The spies were nearly discovered
by soldiers because the king of Jericho had
heard that enemies had entered the city.
He sent troops to search for them, but a
woman called Rahab helped the spies

escape. In return, she asked for their promise that Joshua's army would not harm her family when they invaded, and the spies agreed. Joshua learned about the city and the strength of the mighty walls that surrounded it. He drew up battle plans and prayed to God for help.

Then came the day when Joshua gathered the Israelites on the banks of the River Jordan and commanded everyone to listen carefully. "As soon as the priests carrying the Ark of the Covenant step into the river, the waters will stop flowing," Joshua announced. "As long as they stand holding the Ark in the river, there will be dry land and we will all be able to cross safely to the other side."

To the Israelites' astonishment and joy, it happened exactly as their leader had said. Finally, Joshua's army of forty thousand men stood on a plain in the Promised Land.

The walls of the mighty city of Jericho were thick and high, and the city gates were barred against them. But Joshua listened to God, who told him exactly what to do.

Every day for six days, the Israelite army marched around the city walls. Behind the soldiers, priests equipped with trumpets made of rams' horns carried the Ark of the Covenant.

For Jericho's people it was a terrifying and mysterious display of strength. What

are the Israelites up to they wondered?
Does that Ark really have magical powers?
And why are they marching in that eerie
silence? When will they attack?

Then on the seventh day the silence
ceased and an almighty noise began.
Joshua gave the order for the priests to
blow their horns for all they were worth
as the army marched six times around
the city walls. As they began a seventh
circuit, Joshua signaled for his soldiers to
shout as loud as they could.
Then such a roaring joined
the blaring of the horns
that the walls of Jericho
trembled… and then
shook… and then with

a fearful rumble, collapsed to the ground.
Joshua's army entered the city and
killed every man, woman, and child they
found there—all except for Rahab and
her household, as she had been promised.

Deuteronomy chapter 34; Joshua chapters 1 to 6

Samson
the Strong

The Israelites suffered for many years at the hands of a people called the Philistines. However one day an angel appeared to an Israelite couple and gave a prediction: "You will have a son who will fight for Israel against the Philistines. You must raise him to worship God according to the strict rules of the Nazirite sect, and one of these rules is that you must be careful never to cut his hair."

The couple were overjoyed when they did indeed have a baby boy. They called their little son Samson, but he didn't stay little for long. God ensured that Samson grew up to be tall and strong. He was so strong that once, when he was attacked by a lion, he killed it with his bare hands!

To his parents' immense dismay, Samson fell in love with a Philistine girl, and he insisted on marrying her. At the wedding, Samson set his bride's guests a difficult riddle. They tried for three days to work it out but couldn't come up with the answer. In the end, they pestered the bride to find out, and she persuaded Samson to tell her so she could tell them. Samson realized what his new wife had done. In a temper, he killed thirty Philistines, and stormed off back home. By the time he calmed down and returned to reclaim his bride, she had married someone else! Samson was so furious that he burned the Philistine harvest fields. When the Philistines found out why, they burned down the house of his former bride in turn. With this, Samson's rage knew no bounds and he single-handedly killed many more Philistines before he returned home.

From then on Samson was the Philistines' enemy. They demanded that some Israelites from the tribe of Judah hand him over, or face the consequences. The men explained the situation to Samson, and Samson agreed to be bound and taken to his enemies. But once surrounded, he burst out of his ropes and attacked the Philistines, using a bone as a weapon. He left them all for dead before escaping.

Eventually the giant man became the leader of all Israel. He ruled for twenty years, but the Philistines never gave up trying to capture him. Once, they waited until Samson was in the city of Gaza. They knew he would leave the next morning and planned to attack him by surprise at the city gates. But when they went there at dawn, they found that Samson had outsmarted them. He had left in the middle of the night, uprooting the massive, locked gates and carrying them off!

The Philistines saw yet another chance to take revenge on Samson when he fell in love with a woman called Delilah. Philistine chiefs visited Delilah and promised to pay her five thousand and five hundred pieces of silver if she handed him over to them. So each time Samson visited Delilah, she tested his great strength and tried to persuade him to tell her the secret of it. Eventually, Samson gave in. "My parents promised God that I would never have my hair cut," he explained. "If I cut my hair, I lose God's protection and my strength will be gone."

Delilah's eyes lit up. At last, she knew! Next time Samson came to visit, she gave him wine and gradually he fell asleep. Then she cut off his hair and called the Philistines. It wasn't enough for Samson's enemies to bind him in chains, they blinded him too. Then they threw him in prison and set him to work as a slave.

Around a year passed, and the day came when the Philistines held a great festival in honor of their god, Dagon. The temple was so crowded that three thousand people spilled out onto the roof. There were prayers, songs, dances, poems, and plays. Everyone enjoyed themselves immensely. Then people began shouting for Samson to be brought in, so they could mock the former great Israelite chief.

As the blind man was led into the center of the temple amid jeers, shouts, and insults, no one thought anything of the fact that his hair had grown back. And as the crowd booed, hissed and cursed him, no one heard Samson pray, "Oh God, give me back my strength just one last time." Samson stretched out his hands to his right and left and God helped him find the cold marble of the two main pillars of the temple. Then Samson gave a mighty roar. He pushed and heaved and strained. Amid screams and howls of terror, the huge pillars toppled apart and the temple crashed to the ground in ruins.

And so Samson died, taking thousands of his enemies with him.

Judges chapters 13 to 16

Ruth
the Loyal

Once, there was a terrible famine around Bethlehem. A starving man called Elimelech journeyed with his wife, Naomi, and two sons to live in Moab, where things were better. Then quite suddenly Elimelech died. Naomi and her sons were grief-stricken, but they tried to

carry on as Elimelech would have wanted.
The boys married Moabite girls called Ruth
and Orpah. But then tragedy struck
again—both boys died. Naomi was
heartbroken.

"I am going to return home," Naomi
told Ruth and Orpah, but Ruth refused to
see the old, lonely widow go off on her
own. "Where you go, I go," Ruth vowed.
"Your people will be my people, your god,
my god."

Naomi smiled gratefully through her
tears, and she and Ruth journeyed back to
Bethlehem together.

Ruth and Naomi were now very poor.
They struggled to make a living. One day,
Ruth was in the fields at harvest time,

collecting up the leftover corn when she
caught the eye of the farm-owner, a man
called Boaz. He stopped and asked who she
was. Boaz happened to be a cousin of
Naomi's and he did what he could to help
Ruth. Boaz told her she was welcome in his
fields all the time. He told his harvesters to
let her drink from their water jars whenever
she wanted. He even invited Ruth to join
his harvesters for a meal, giving her enough
food to take home for supper. Boaz also
secretly told his harvesters to leave extra
corn behind so Ruth would have more to
pick up.

Day after day, Boaz showed Ruth small
kindnesses like these, and eventually Naomi
dared to send Ruth to ask Boaz formally

for his protection.

Boaz was delighted. As was tradition, he went to the city gate and declared in public that he wanted to look after Ruth and Naomi. Boaz and Ruth were married, and Boaz cared for the women all their lives.

So Ruth was rewarded for her loyalty and kindness to Naomi, and Naomi was comforted in her old age. In the fullness of time, God sent Ruth a baby boy, Obed, who brought the two women happiness. They never dreamed that Obed would have a son called Jesse, who would have a son called David, who would one day become the greatest king Israel ever had.

Ruth chapters 1 to 4

David and the Giant

The people of Israel saw that other nations had kings to rule them and demanded that they should have one too. The great prophet Samuel asked God for approval. He was told to choose a man called Saul from the tribe of Benjamin to be the first king of Israel.

King Saul won many victories against Israel's enemies, but he did not always do as God wanted. For this reason, God told Samuel that Saul's sons would never be king. God ordered that Samuel travel to Bethlehem and find a shepherd boy called David, the youngest son of a man called Jesse. It was David that God wanted to be the next king. Samuel did so, and gave David a special blessing, and from then on God was always with him.

King Saul's army often had to fight the Philistines because they were constantly invading Israelite territory. Every Israelite who could be spared was called to defend their lands, and three of Jesse's other sons went to the frontline. One day, Jesse sent

David off with food supplies for them. He reached the camp as a battle was beginning and the armored soldiers were marching onto the battlefield. Suddenly, they all turned and came running back in fear.

"Whatever is going on?" David called as one terrified soldier ran past.

The man just shouted, "Look!" and pointed behind him.

Striding out in front of the Philistine army was a warrior more enormous than David could have dreamed. He was almost twice as big as everyone else!

"Run away if you like," the giant bellowed.

158

"There's no need to do battle if you're too cowardly. Just send someone to fight me in single combat. Whoever wins has victory for their side. Now, is any one of you men big enough to take up the challenge?" He smashed his mighty spear against his shield and threw back his head and roared, and the noise crashed around the surrounding hills like thunder.

David was outraged. "How dare he! It's an insult not just to us but to God!" he spat. "Just let me at him! Out in the pastures, I've killed lions and bears when they've attacked my father's flocks and I can do the same to this beast too! God protected me then as He will protect me now."

"Well…" said Saul, casting around for

other volunteers. None were forthcoming.
"Very well, and God be with you." Saul
insisted on dressing David in his own
armor, but it was so big and bulky that he
couldn't move, so David took it off again.
He strode out to meet the giant, Goliath of
Gath, with just his staff, his slingshot, and
five smooth stones in his shepherd's pouch.

King Saul and his army watched in
amazement. The giant was roaring with
laughter as a mere child walked toward
him. The young boy was yelling back that
he was going to slay Goliath in the name of
God. The shepherd boy stood firm as the
giant ran toward him with death in his
eyes, brandishing his spear. Then David
raised his slingshot and whirled it around

once… A stone struck Goliath in the forehead, sending him crashing to the ground, dead. As King Saul and his army cheered, David drew the giant's sword and cut off Goliath's head with one blow. And the Philistines turned and fled, leaving the Israelites triumphant.

I Samuel chapters 8, 9, 16, 17

Solomon
the Wise

When Saul, the first king of Israel died, David came to the throne, just as God had wanted. It was King David who made Israel a great, unified nation with Jerusalem as its capital city. He had the Ark of the Covenant brought there amid great rejoicing. He wanted to build a glorious temple to house it, but God told David that He was going to entrust that job to his son, Solomon, the third king of Israel.

Solomon was in his early twenties when he took over the throne. He was determined to carry on his father's good work, strengthening the nation, and keeping peace with Israel's enemies, but he wasn't sure exactly how to do it. He felt he lacked the experience and confidence he needed to be a good king.

One night, God appeared to Solomon in a dream and asked how He could help. "Please, God, give me the gift of wisdom," the king begged.

God was delighted. Solomon could have asked for gold or a long life or power over his enemies, or a whole range of other selfish things. Wisdom to govern the people well was an excellent choice and God was only too happy to oblige.

Not long afterward, two women who were in the middle of a bitter argument were brought before Solomon so he could settle their dispute. The women lived together and both had recently given birth to a child. However, one of the babies had died, and now each woman was claiming the living baby as hers.

"It's her baby who died," the first one insisted to Solomon. "Do you think I don't know my own child?"

"No, her baby died!" the second woman protested. "Then she stole mine."

Solomon signaled for the women to be quiet. After a few minutes he announced, "Bring me my sword!" As the weapon was fetched he continued, "Cut the child in two and give half to each woman!"

"Yes, neither of us should have him!" cried one woman.

But the other burst out wailing. "Sire, please! I would rather see him given away to her than for him to be hurt!"

Then Solomon knew who the real mother of the baby was. And all the people of Israel knew that such wisdom could only have come from God.

II Samuel chapters 5 to 7; I Kings chapters 1, 3

Solomon the Magnificent

The nation of Israel prospered under King Solomon. He kept peace in his lands and trading routes thrived as merchants could travel in safety. He ruled wisely and well, stunning everyone with his incredible knowledge. Then Solomon began to fulfil his father's dream of building a glorious temple, just as God had said he would. After nearly five hundred years, the Ark of the Covenant was to have a home.

Solomon drafted thousands of workers to build the temple. It was made from beautiful cedar wood, which came from the lands of a friend of his, King Hiram of Tyre in Lebanon. Solomon wanted to use only the finest materials and the newest, most exciting techniques, even if it meant going to great lengths and expense to bring materials and craftspeople from abroad. Laborers spent years building massive stone pillars, carving enormous doors and wooden wall panels with angels and intricate flowers, dying and weaving beautiful curtains, and lining whole rooms with gold, which were then decorated with stunning jewels.

The day finally came when Solomon ordered the temple to be filled with treasures and the Ark of the Covenant brought to its new home. It was done with such procession and celebrating that no one had ever seen anything like it. As the priests were leaving the temple, the building was suddenly filled with a blazing light so bright that no one could look at it. The king stood in front of the altar before all of his people and gave thanks to God, praying

that He would always be with the nation of
Israel. Then began a week of feasting.

Solomon didn't stop his building plans at
the temple. He erected a magnificent palace
and splendid buildings in Jerusalem and
Canaan. Rulers from far-off countries
traveled to see the marvels for themselves.
Even the Queen of Sheba made a journey
of fifteen hundred miles through the desert
in a camel train laden down with spices,
jewels, and gold. The queen was amazed—
not just by Solomon's incredible buildings
but by the wisdom with which he ran the
country. "Praise be to your God," she
exclaimed, "for He must be hugely pleased
with what you have done in His honor."

I Kings chapters 4 to 8, 10

Jonah and the Giant Fish

One day, God told a man called Jonah, "Go to Assyria, to the capital city of Nineveh. Tell the wicked people there about me and make sure they change their sinful ways."

Now Jonah didn't care for these people and wasn't much bothered if they found out about God or not. He also didn't like the sound of walking into the capital city of a powerful, warlike nation and telling the people what they were doing wrong. So Jonah got on a boat in the opposite direction to Nineveh, heading for Spain.

As soon as the ship was on its way, God sent a mighty storm its way. The sailors were terrified and began praying to be saved. Still the rain lashed the boat and the wind and waves hurled it this way and that. Then the sailors decided that someone on board must be cursed. They drew lots

and came up with Jonah's name.
Shamefully, Jonah confessed that he
was disobeying God by being on the boat.
"You'll have to throw me overboard," he
wept, "it's the only way you'll get this
storm to stop." The sailors were
horrified and did their best to row to
shore. But when the storm grew even
worse they concluded there was only
one thing for it—and dropped Jonah
into the water.

The minute they did so, the wind
dropped, the rain stopped, the waves died
away, and the ship was saved. God saved
Jonah too. Instead of letting him sink and
drown, He sent a massive fish that
swallowed him. For three days Jonah

wallowed in the stinky darkness of the fish's belly, praying to God for another chance. Finally, to his relief, the fish spat him out onto a sandy shore.

"Go to Nineveh," God said again, "and give the people my message. If they don't change their behavior, I will destroy the city after forty days."

This time Jonah did what he was told. To his immense surprise the Assyrians listened. The king of Nineveh believed God's threat and ordered his people to mend their ways. Soon, there was a drop in crime. People started being more polite and kind to each other. They prayed for forgiveness and fasted, and started worshiping God. The forty days came and went and God left the city and its people untouched.

Jonah stomped off on his own into the countryside. "I knew this would happen!" he moaned to God, sitting down in protest. "I've come all this way—nearly drowned, been eaten by a fish, then walked for miles to face crowds of hostile strangers—and all for nothing. You haven't punished anyone or destroyed anything at all."

God decided to teach the angry man a lesson. He made a tree shoot up swiftly right where Jonah was sitting, so all day he could rest in its cool shade. However the next day, God sent insects to eat the tree so it shriveled and died, leaving Jonah sitting in the blazing sun. God also sent desert wind to roast him. "If only my poor tree hadn't died!" Jonah groaned.

"Well," said God kindly, "if you're upset about a tree—a tree that you neither planted nor looked after—how upset do you think I would have been if the city of Nineveh had been lost? One hundred and twenty thousand people live there, not to mention all the animals."

And Jonah finally understood that God cared for all people, not just the Israelites— and for animals too. After all, hadn't God made them in the first place?

Jonah

Daniel in the Lions' Den

Daniel was such an outstanding advisor that King Darius of the Medes and Persians put him in charge of his whole empire. The other officials were so jealous that they came up with an idea that was certain to land Daniel in trouble. They suggested to Darius that he should order that no one pray to anyone but him for thirty days. If anyone disobeyed, they were to be thrown into a pit of hungry lions. The king thought it was a great idea and signed the order.

Now Daniel was a good, holy man. Of course, he continued to pray to God three times a day, as always in front of his window in full view of passersby.

It wasn't long before his enemies reported him to the king. Darius was devastated, but he could not go back on his word. He ordered that Daniel should be thrown to the lions. "May your god save you," the king prayed, and a huge stone was placed over the pit so there was no way Daniel could escape.

Darius spent all night thinking how he had caused Daniel to be flung to the lions. As soon as dawn came he hurried to the pit and called, "Daniel! Was God with you? Are you still alive?"

To Darius' relief, Daniel answered, "Yes, sire. God sent an angel to guard me and the lions have left me untouched."

The king set Daniel free, and all the people who had accused him were thrown into the pit. The lions tore them to bits until nothing but bones were left.

Daniel chapter 6

Queen Esther
the Brave

King Xerxes was a mighty Persian king
whose empire stretched from India to
Ethiopia. He was once so displeased with
his wife, Vashti, that he announced she was
no longer his queen. He ordered for
beautiful young women to be brought from
all corners of his empire to the palace so he

could choose a new wife.

One of the men who worked in the royal household was an old Jew called Mordecai. He urged his adopted daughter Esther to go to the palace and take part in the beauty competition. Mordecai warned her not to tell anyone she was his daughter or that she was Jewish, for many people hated the captives who had been brought from Israel.

Esther did as she was told and went to the palace. For a year she was pampered with beauty treatments, and had lessons in grooming and how to behave like a queen. When all the candidates were presented to the king, Xerxes chose Esther as his queen. He soon found that she wasn't just a pretty face either. He came to like her very much.

One day, she told him how Mordecai had overheard two servants plotting to kill him, and Xerxes believed Esther at once. He had the two men arrested and hanged, and ordered for the event to be written down in his official Book of Records. Mordecai and Esther had saved his life.

Some time later, King Xerxes made a man called Haman his chief minister and commanded his subjects to bow before him. Mordecai always refused. "I bow to none other than God," the old man would insist. This disobedience drove Haman quite mad. He was determined to have revenge. Not just on Mordecai, but on all Jewish people. He told the king that the Jews were disobedient and nothing but trouble, and that his kingdom would be better off if he had them all put to death. "Whatever you think best," Xerxes told his trusted minister, and gave Haman his royal seal to sign the execution warrant.

When Mordecai found out he was appalled, and begged Esther to ask Xerxes for mercy. She dressed in her finest robes and went unsummoned into the king's presence, an action for which the law said she could have been put to death. Luckily, the king was happy to see her and said she could have whatever she had come for.

"All I would like is for you and Haman to be my guests at dinner tomorrow," Esther said charmingly, and the king agreed.

Esther held a wonderful dinner for the

men, with delicious food and witty conversation in beautiful surroundings. Having begun to win her husband and his minister over, she invited them to another dinner the following night, when she hoped she could finish the job and ask for forgiveness for the Jews. Little did she know that later that very evening Haman had ordered that a gallows be built at the palace. They were to hang the man he hated—Mordecai, her father.

At around the same time, Xerxes was being read aloud to from the Book of Records. The reader happened to announce the entry that described how Mordecai had helped foil the earlier plot to kill King Xerxes, and it reminded the king that he had never honored the man.

Just then, a servant announced that Haman was asking to see him. He had come to ask for the king's permission to execute Mordecai.

"Now Haman, tell me what you would do to reward a man you wanted to honor," wondered the king, as his chief minister was ushered in.

Haman tried to hide a smug smirk. He thought that he must be the man the king wanted to honor. "Such a person should be dressed in robes fit for a king and paraded on one of your own horses through the streets as a hero," Haman sighed.

"What a good idea!" Xerxes said, delighted. "Then that's what I want you to do for Mordecai the Jew in the morning."

Haman was outraged, yet he had no choice but to do as the king had commanded. By the time he arrived at Esther's second supper, Haman's face was as sulky and ugly as Esther's was beautiful.

This time, the queen begged Xerxes for mercy. She confessed that she was a Jew and that orders had been given for all Jewish people to be put to death.

"Who has dared to do such a terrible thing?" boomed the king, outraged.

"The man who is sitting beside you," Esther said quietly. "Haman."

Xerxes was so choked with fury that he couldn't speak and he strode out into the palace gardens.

He returned to find his chief minister at
Esther's feet, grabbing at her skirt. Haman
was in fact begging for
mercy, but it looked as
though he was
attacking the
king's wife. To
make matters
worse, one of

Esther's servants told the king that Haman had built a gallows to kill Mordecai, the very man who had once helped save Xerxes's life.

The king did not delay in having Haman executed on his own gallows. Then he sent letters throughout his empire, ordering that the Jews should be respected, and allowed to defend themselves if necessary.

And that is how the brave, beautiful Esther saved her people, the Jews.

Esther chapters 1 to 8

THE NEW TESTAMENT

The Angel Gabriel
Brings News

There once lived in Galilee an old priest called Zachariah and his wife Elisabeth. Both were good Jewish people who always tried to live by God's rules. However, they were sad because they had never been able to have children.

One day Zachariah was given a special

honor. It was his turn to go into the great temple in Jerusalem, to the most sacred altar, and make an offering to God. As he did so, deep in prayer, an angel suddenly appeared. Zachariah was terrified.

"Don't be afraid," the angel said. "I have come with great news. God is going to answer the prayers of you and your wife, begging for children. He is going to give you a son. God wants you to call him John. Your son is going to be a very holy man and will do great work for Him."

Zachariah was stunned. Was he really seeing and hearing an angel? And even if he was, Elisabeth was past the usual age for having children. "Are you sure?" he asked in disbelief. "How can this be?"

"I am Gabriel,
a messenger
from God!"
the angel
said sternly.
"Because you
haven't believed me
you will stay silent until it
comes true!" And the angel
disappeared, just as suddenly as
he had arrived.

Imagine Elisabeth's surprise when her
husband came home unable to speak. He
had to explain what had happened by
acting things out and writing things down.
Imagine Elisabeth's amazement when a
short while later her husband's prediction

194

came true and she found that she was
pregnant. Elisabeth was astonished when six
months later, her younger cousin Mary
arrived unannounced. All at once Elisabeth
knew that Mary was also having a
baby—a very special baby indeed.

Just as mysteriously, Mary knew about
Elisabeth's baby. Bursting with excitement
and happiness, she explained everything to
her cousin. Mary had been going about her
chores one day as usual when suddenly the
angel Gabriel appeared in her little home in
the town of Nazareth. It was he who had
told her that Elisabeth was going to have a
baby. But the angel had even more
important news for Mary. Gabriel told her
that God thought she was very special and

that He was going to make her the mother of His son. Mary was going to have a little boy, and God wanted Mary to call him Jesus. "He will be ruler over all the Lord's people and His Kingdom will have no end," the angel told the stunned woman.

Mary hurried off to visit Elisabeth straight away so she could share her joy with her cousin. She stayed as long as she could to help the older lady through her pregnancy. But before Elisabeth's baby was born, Mary had to return home to prepare for the birth of her own child.

Luke chapter 1

His Name
is John

The day came when Elisabeth gave
birth to a baby boy just as the angel
Gabriel had said. Her neighbors and
relatives came to admire the new arrival.
Everyone marveled at what a miracle it was
that Elisabeth had been able to have a baby
at her age.

When the baby was one week old, the
family held a party to promise him to God
and to officially name him. Everyone
assumed that the couple were going to call
the boy Zachariah because it was tradition
for the first son to be named after his father.
Elisabeth caused a stir when she announced
that the baby was to be named John.

"John!" Elisabeth's relations exclaimed.
"There's no one in our family called John.
Where on earth have you come up with
that name from?" Turning to Zachariah,
they asked, "Zachariah, you want your son
to be named after you, don't you? Of
course you do! Tell Elisabeth immediately."

Poor Zachariah still couldn't speak. Very
frustrated, he signaled around for something

to write with. Someone hurried to find him a writing tablet. Then Zachariah wrote the biggest, boldest letters he could fit on the tablet and then held it up so everyone could see. It read: HIS NAME IS JOHN.

Everyone grumbled, but in the midst of their murmurings Zachariah suddenly found he could speak again. "My voice has come back!" he cried. "Thank you, God, for everything you have done for us!"

It wasn't long before the news of what had happened at the party had spread far and wide.

Luke chapter 1

199

The Birth
of Jesus

Mary was engaged to marry a young man called Joseph, a local carpenter. When she told Joseph she was expecting a baby he was very upset. The baby couldn't be his because they weren't married. And in those days, if an unmarried woman was expecting a baby it was quite shameful.

However, Joseph had a dream in which an angel told him, "Don't be afraid to take Mary as your wife. Her baby is the Son of God Himself. The prophets of long ago foretold that He would come and save everyone from their sins. Raise Him as your own son. God wants you to call Him Jesus." After this Joseph felt much better. He realized he would be honored to bring the little boy up as his own, and he and Mary were married straight away.

However, near the time that the baby was to be born, another problem arose. The emperor Augustus Caesar ordered a survey of all the people in his lands. He commanded that every man had to travel to where he was born, taking his family with him to have their names put on a register. Joseph had been born in the city of Bethlehem in Judea, in the south of the country, which was quite a distance from the village of Nazareth. Mary was heavily pregnant and traveling would be very difficult for her. Nevertheless, the couple did not have a choice. They packed what they would need for the trip and set off. Mary couldn't possibly walk all that way, so she rode on a donkey. It was a bumpy and tiring journey for a woman so close to having a baby.

By the time the couple

reached Bethlehem they were exhausted, hungry, and dusty. Joseph began trying to find a room in which they could stay. He trudged with the donkey and Mary from one lodging place to the next. But to the couple's dismay, everywhere was full. The city was bustling with travelers who had come to register for the emperor's survey.

As they were turned away from one place after another, Mary began to feel that the baby was on its way. Hurriedly, Joseph banged on the door of the nearest inn. After a few moments, the busy innkeeper peered outside. "Don't bother asking, we're full," he said, as soon as he saw the travelers.

"Wait, please help us!" cried Joseph, stopping the innkeeper from shutting the door on them. "My wife's about to have a baby. She can't give birth out here in the street! Haven't you got a spare corner somewhere you could squeeze us in?"

"Well…" said the innkeeper, looking at poor Mary in pain on the donkey. "I haven't got a single room to spare, but you're welcome to shelter in my stable if you don't mind the animals."

"Thank you, thank you so much," Joseph said, gratefully shaking the man's hand, and the innkeeper showed them the way to his stable.

It was there, with the donkeys, oxen, and sheep looking on, that Mary gave birth to the baby boy who was to be the savior of the world. She wrapped Him up in cloths

and nestled Him in a manger full of straw.
And baby Jesus was warm and safe, with
His mother and foster father by His side.

Matthew chapter 1; Luke chapter 2

The Shepherds' Visit

On the night that Jesus was born, the city of Bethlehem throbbed with people, while the surrounding countryside was peaceful except for a few shepherds and their flocks. The shepherds were taking turns at sleeping and watching. They made sure that the sheep weren't wandering away and kept watch for hungry wolves.

All at once the starry night sky above the shepherds blazed as bright as day. Then it blazed brighter still, too bright for the shepherds to look up. They shielded their eyes from the blinding glare as an angel appeared high overhead. The shepherds were terrified.

"Don't be afraid," came the angel's voice, clear through the still, cold night. "I bring you

wonderful news—wonderful news for everyone on Earth. This very night a child has been born who will be the savior of all people. You can find Him in a stable in Bethlehem,

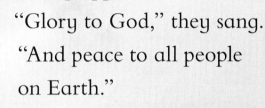

lying in a manger."

The air was filled with singing more beautiful than the shepherds had ever heard, as hundreds of thousands of angels suddenly appeared in the heavens.

"Glory to God," they sang. "And peace to all people on Earth."

The shepherds stood transfixed until the angels had finished their song. Then the heavenly music died and the angels faded away.

Could it really be true the shepherds wondered? In ancient stories prophets had predicted for hundreds of years that a man would come who would save everyone from

their sins. They called him the Messiah. Maybe he had really come at last.

The shepherds hurried off to Bethlehem, to see for themselves. They searched through the streets until they heard the sound of a newborn baby crying from a stable behind an inn. There they found Mary and Joseph looking after baby Jesus. In great excitement, they told the startled couple all that they had seen and heard. Mary fell very quiet, taking it all in.

The shepherds stayed for a while, marveling at the baby boy who they had been told was the Messiah, but they had to return to their flocks. All the way back they couldn't stop talking about the amazing chorus of angels and how their words had come true. They told everyone they met, praising God, and giving thanks for all that they had seen and been told.

Luke chapter 2

A Special Day for Simeon and Anna

When Jesus was one week old, Mary and Joseph held the usual ceremony to promise their son to God and officially name Him. They also made a trip from Bethlehem to Jerusalem. It was traditional for Jewish families to take their first son to the temple there to give thanks to God and make a sacrifice of two doves or pigeons.

In Jerusalem there lived an old man whose name was Simeon. He was a holy man and had always tried his best to live a good life. God had promised Simeon a reward for his lifetime of faithful service. He promised that he would not die without seeing the Messiah, who was to save the world. For years Simeon longed for this wonderful day to come.

On the morning when Mary and Joseph brought Jesus into the temple, Simeon was already there. God's Holy Spirit had spoken to him earlier, telling him that the day had finally arrived. Simeon hurried to the temple straight away. As soon as the old man caught sight of the tiny baby, he immediately knew who He was.

"Thanks be to God," he cried, taking the little bundle in his arms. "Now I can die in peace because I have seen the savior who will bring glory to Israel and spread the Word of God to everyone on Earth." Mary and Joseph were amazed.

"Your little child is a sign from God," Simeon continued, "but many people won't believe what He says and will turn against Him." Simeon looked at Mary with great pity in his eyes. "Because of this, great sorrow will one day pierce your heart like a sword."

Just then an old woman who visited the temple every day came shuffling over. Her name was Anna and she was a prophetess.

"Can I see my savior?" she asked. By now, people had begun to crowd around to see what was going on. As Mary and Joseph showed Jesus to Anna, she started telling everyone how the baby came from God and was the hope of the world.

When Mary and Joseph finally left the temple that day, they couldn't help but feel overwhelmed by the amazing events that were happening.

Luke chapter 2

Follow
the Star

Far away in distant lands to the east,
there lived some wise men who were
astrologers. Every night they gazed up at
the sky and studied the stars, trying to work
out what their movements around the
heavens meant for people on Earth. One
night they were stunned by a brand new

star that appeared much bigger
and brighter than the rest. They
hurried to consult their ancient
books to see what it could mean.
The wise men became very excited by
what they found, and were in no doubt that
a great Jewish prophecy had come true.
The star was a sign that a baby had been
born who would become the king of God's
Chosen People. The wise men decided to set
off to find him at once. They packed up
their camels with supplies and set off into
the desert, heading in the direction of the
star that blazed each night in the sky. They
arrived in the city of Jerusalem.

News soon reached King Herod of Judea
that strangers from the east had arrived in

Jerusalem. These strangers were searching for a newborn baby they were calling the "King of the Jews." Of course Herod didn't like the sound of that at all. As far as he was concerned he had been crowned King of the Jews and he wanted it to stay that way. He certainly wasn't going to put up with rumors spreading about a rival—who fulfilled one of the ancient prophecies no less. It would just stir up trouble among the people and they might rise up against him.

King Herod set about dealing with the problem in his cold, calculated way. First, he called a meeting of all the chief Jewish religious leaders to find out more. "Where do your ancient books say the Messiah is to be born?" he asked, innocently.

"In Bethlehem," the holy men answered.

Then King Herod called his guards and ordered them to find the wise men and bring them to him. "But do it in secret," he commanded. "I don't want people to get the impression that I think these men and their rumors are important."

The wise men were nervous when they were summoned to see the king. They had heard that Herod could be a cruel leader. However, they were surprised to find him most polite, interested, and even helpful in their quest. "The Jewish elders have told me that you shouldn't be looking in Jerusalem," he explained. "Try Bethlehem instead. When you have found the future king, do come back and tell me all about it.

I'd like to go and pay my respects too."

The wise men had no idea that King Herod only wanted to know where the baby was so he could have him killed.

They set off to Bethlehem and followed the star to where it appeared to hang biggest and brightest in the sky, over the house in

which Mary and Joseph were now staying.
The wise men were surprised to find the
baby in an ordinary home rather than a
splendid palace. They bowed to worship
Him and presented Mary and Joseph with
gifts—jeweled gold caskets, and the rare
spices frankincense and myrrh.

Herod never got to hear of the wise
men's success. The night before they were
due to set off home, they had a troubling
dream that warned them not to return to
the king. The wise men took a different
route back to their lands in the east and
Herod never found them.

Matthew chapter 2

Flight from Danger

After the wise men had visited Jesus, an angel appeared to Joseph in a dream. "Herod is trying to find the baby to kill Him," the angel warned. "Take Him and Mary to Egypt. It will be a long, hard journey, but it will take you safely out of the cruel king's reach. Stay there until I tell you it is safe to return."

Joseph woke up with a start. He woke Mary and told her to make ready to travel straight away. The family hurried through the dark, sleeping streets of Bethlehem and onto the road to Egypt.

Meanwhile back in Jerusalem, Herod was waiting for the wise men to return from Bethlehem and tell him where the baby king of kings was. He waited… and waited… Eventually he realized that the wise men weren't coming—he had been tricked! Herod flew into a fury and roared at his army chief, "Send your men to search every house in Bethlehem.

223

I want every boy under two years of age put to death immediately!"

By the time the soldiers arrived in Bethlehem to carry out their terrible task, Jesus, Mary, and Joseph were miles away in Egypt. They stayed there for several months until an angel appeared to Joseph once more, telling him that King Herod had died and it was safe to go back to Israel. However Joseph did not take his family back to Bethlehem. The city was far too close to Jerusalem, where King Herod's son was now on the throne. Instead, he traveled north back to their home in the sleepy town of Nazareth in the remote area of Galilee.

Matthew chapter 2

Jesus in the Temple

Every year at the festival of Passover, all Jewish men went to visit the temple in Jerusalem, to pray and give thanks to God. Joseph always went and, like many women, Mary went too. Of course the number of people who crowded into the city was huge. The lodging houses were heaving, people packed streets and the temple itself was totally crammed. Like many parents with young children, Mary and Joseph left Jesus with a relative or neighbor when they went to celebrate the festival. But when He reached the age of twelve, they decided Jesus was old enough to go with them.

The family traveled to Jerusalem with a large group of relatives and friends. When the festival was over, they all set off to travel home. Joseph walked with the men, Mary chatted to the women, and Jesus ran back and forth with the other children.

But at the end of the first day's journey, when the group of travelers began to make camp for the night, Jesus had disappeared. Mary and Joseph called for their son at the tops of their voices, but He didn't come. With a rising sense of panic, the couple dashed up and down, describing Jesus to everyone and asking if anyone had seen Him. No one had. Darkness was drawing in fast. "There's nothing else we can do tonight, but as soon as it gets light tomorrow we'll retrace our steps and find Him," Joseph comforted his weeping wife.

Of course, Mary and Joseph didn't sleep for worrying about where Jesus was and whether He was safe. At sunrise Mary and Joseph began making their way back to Jerusalem, asking everyone they met if they had seen a lost twelve-year-old boy. They reached the city and hunted around its bustling streets for two days, but there was no sign of Him.

The third day came and in desperation Mary and Joseph went to look in the great temple itself. To their astonishment, there they found Jesus deep in discussion with a group of Jewish priests and leaders.

228

"Your son has such a wise understanding of the ancient writings, we can't believe He is only twelve," the holy men told Mary and Joseph. "He asks questions that most people never think to ask, and He's been giving us answers too!"

But Mary and Joseph just wanted to know what had happened to Jesus. "Where on earth have you been?" They cried. "We've been worried sick!"

Jesus replied calmly, "You should have known that you would find me in my Father's house."

Luke chapter 2

John the Baptist

Elisabeth and Zachariah's son John grew up to be a holy man. He went to live on his own in the countryside of Judea, so he could think about God and pray without being distracted. He wore only a simple robe woven from camel hair and survived by eating locusts and wild honey. When he was about thirty years old, he began preaching to anyone he came across. "Be sorry for your sins and turn away from evil," was his message, "so you can enter God's Kingdom, which is nearly here!"

John was such a powerful speaker that people traveled especially to see him. People from all walks of life flocked from towns, villages, and the city of Jerusalem too. From poor common people, to powerful Jewish groups such as the Pharisees and the Sadducees, as well as farmers, shopkeepers, tax collectors, and even Roman soldiers. They usually found John on the banks of the River Jordan.

"What does God want from us?" they would ask.

John would advise, "Be kind and generous. Treat each other fairly. Don't hurt anyone, neither in your actions nor words."

John's teachings were so stirring that people often asked him if he was the savior—the Messiah spoken of in the ancient writings. "No," John would insist, "but I am trying to prepare the way for His coming."

One after the other, people would tell John all the things they had done wrong in their lives, hanging their heads in shame. They felt truly sorry for their sins and promised they wouldn't do them again, and that they would turn to God and try to live by His rules. Then John baptized them in the holy river. He dipped the people into

the water and gave them God's blessing, so
their sins were washed away and they could
begin afresh. "I'm only baptizing you with
water," John told them, "but the man who
is coming will baptize you with the fire of
the Holy Spirit. He is so holy that I am not
even good enough to undo his sandals."

One day, among the crowd on the banks
of the Jordan, Jesus was waiting to be
baptized. John knew who He was
immediately. "It's not right that I baptize
you," John told Jesus. "You should be
baptizing me."

But Jesus insisted that it was what God
wanted. So together the men walked into
the river. As soon as John had baptized
Jesus, the clouds above them parted and

light blazed down on Jesus. A dove came gliding down and hovered above Jesus, and John knew that it was God's Holy Spirit coming down to Him. Then a voice spoke into everyone's minds saying, "This is my beloved son, with whom I am very pleased."

Matthew chapter 3; Mark chapter 1; Luke chapter 3; John chapter 1

Jesus is Tempted

Jesus went into the desert lands of Judea so He could think undisturbed about God and what He wanted Him to do. Jesus was all alone except for the wild animals. He prayed for forty days and forty nights, until He was weak with tiredness and hunger. Then the devil came to Jesus in His thoughts, trying to tempt Him into committing a sin.

"If you really are the Son of God," said the devil, "turn these stones into bread."

But Jesus refused to do so. He had heard God call Him His son when John baptized Him. He didn't need to work a miracle to prove it, and He knew it would be wrong to do so just to make life easier. Even though Jesus felt like fainting through hunger, He trusted God to look after him.

The devil was angry, and he tried again. He made Jesus feel as though He was standing on the roof of the great temple in Jerusalem, looking down on the bustling courtyards below. "Announce to everyone that you are the Son of God," the devil

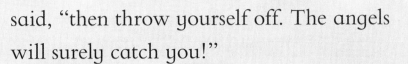

said, "then throw yourself off. The angels will surely catch you!"

But Jesus refused to do so again. He knew it would be wrong to test God in this way. And God wanted to win followers because people loved Him, not just because they'd seen a miracle.

The devil was bursting with fury but he refused to give up. He tried for a third time to get Jesus to sin. The devil made Jesus feel as if He was standing on top of a very high mountain. When He looked down He could see all the countries of the world spread out beneath Him.

"Look," whispered the devil in Jesus' ear. "This is what I can give you—all the lands and peoples from one end of the Earth to

the other—if you will just bow down and
worship me."
Jesus knew that a lot of people
had turned to wickedness in order to
make themselves powerful rulers.
But the kingdoms the devil
helped them establish were
full of cruelty and misery.
Moreover, Jesus knew that
only one kingdom would
last forever—the
Kingdom of God.

"No! Get away from me!" roared Jesus. "I will only worship God."

The devil was defeated and he crept away. As Jesus sank down, utterly exhausted, angels came to look after Him.

Matthew chapter 4; Mark chapter 1; Luke chapter 4

Jesus' First
Miracle

Jesus left the River Jordan and the desert lands of Judea in the south behind Him and went back to live in Galilee in the north. He knew God wanted Him to begin teaching everyone what they had to do to enter His Kingdom. Several followers of John the Baptist went with Jesus to help.

Jesus preached in Jewish places of worship called synagogues. "Beg God to forgive your sins," He told everyone, just like John the Baptist had, "so you can enter the Kingdom of God, which is coming." News soon spread that Jesus was an exciting speaker and He quickly built a following.

Not long after Jesus had arrived back in Galilee, His mother Mary told Him that they had been invited to a wedding in Cana. It was to be a big event and the wedding celebrations were set to go on for several days.

Sitting down at the feast for the wedding everyone was having a wonderful time. About halfway through, Mary noticed that the wine was starting to run out. She knew

241

it would be highly embarrassing for the bride and bridegroom if they couldn't offer their guests any more to drink. So she whispered to Jesus, feeling sure that He could help.

"I'm sorry but I can't do anything about it," Jesus whispered back. "It's not a good time right now."

But Mary turned to the flustered servants and said, "I've noticed that you are low on wine, but my son can help. Do exactly what He says."

Jesus sighed. He gave his mother a gentle smile. Then He told the servants, "Fill all the empty wine jars up to the brim with water." They hurried to do as He said. "Now pour some into a goblet and take it to your boss, the steward, for tasting," Jesus instructed. They did so, rather worried, but to their astonishment the steward smacked his lips, clapped his hands and ordered it to be served to the guests at once. The water had turned into wine. Not only that, but excellent wine—better than they had previously been serving. The steward strode straight over to the bridegroom to congratulate him on his good taste and generosity.

Through the power of God His Father, Jesus had performed His first miracle. There were many more to come.

Matthew chapter 4; Mark chapter 1; Luke chapter 4; John chapters 1, 2

Jesus Goes
Fishing

Jesus sailed out on the Sea of Galilee in a
boat belonging to two of His followers,
Peter and Andrew who were fishermen.
"Throw your nets into the water. Let's see if
there are any fish today," Jesus suggested.

"We already know there aren't," Peter
replied gloomily. "We were fishing all last

night and we didn't catch a thing."

"Well, why not try again?" Jesus urged.

"I don't think there's much point," Peter shrugged. Then he saw a strange gleam in Jesus' eyes. "But I suppose there's no harm in having another go."

He and Andrew lowered their nets and waited... Then after a while, the brothers went to lift them up again. To their astonishment, the nets were so heavy with fish that they couldn't raise them. The stunned pair had to signal for help from a nearby boat, belonging to the two sons of a man called Zebedee. Their names were James and John and they rowed over to help.

Jesus watched the four men work hard together. It took all their strength to heave

245

the enormous catch aboard. Soon Peter's
and Andrew's little boat was full of shiny,
wriggling fish, and so weighed down in the
water that it was in danger of sinking.

The men knew that this sort of catch was unheard of. Something miraculous must have happened. Peter fell on his knees before Jesus and said, "Lord, I'm not good enough to be one of your followers. I shouldn't have doubted what you said, I should have just done it straight away."

"Don't worry," Jesus said, kindly. "Anyway, I'm going to show you how to catch people instead of fish…"

From then on, Peter, Andrew, James, and John stayed at Jesus' side and helped him.

Matthew chapter 4; Mark chapter 1; Luke chapter 5

Jesus Chooses Special Helpers

Jesus became so well known that He couldn't go anywhere without being surrounded by crowds. He once climbed high up a mountain so He could be on His own. Jesus prayed to God all night. When He came down the next day, He summoned twelve men from His many disciples.

They were brothers Peter and Andrew, brothers James and John, a former follower of John the Baptist called Philip, Matthew the tax collector, a man called Simon who was a member of a Jewish group called the Zealots, a second James, and four others—Thomas, Bartholomew, Thaddaeus, and Judas Iscariot.

Jesus took the twelve men to one side and spoke to them. "I want you to be my special helpers," He explained. "I want each of you to go and preach to people what I have preached. I am going to give you the power to heal the sick, just as I do. Don't accept any money for it. Don't take anything on your travels except for the clothes you are wearing, just live off people's kindness. It won't be easy—some people will ignore you, others will try to stop you spreading my message and some may even try to have you killed. But God will always be with you, looking after you, and His Holy Spirit will give you courage. And if you give up your life for me, I promise you will have a new and happier life in Heaven."

So for several weeks, the twelve men went out around the countryside, teaching and healing in Jesus' name.

Matthew chapter 10; Mark chapters 3, 6; Luke chapters 6, 9

Jesus the Healer

Soon people from far and wide came to hear about Jesus. Men, women, and children were excited by the sound of this captivating preacher who worked miracles. They began seeking Jesus out, traveling to wherever He was to see Him for themselves. Jesus tried to help as many people as He could and convince them to turn to God.

After Jesus had preached in one place, a man who was suffering from the terrible skin disease leprosy crept up to Him. He was extremely nervous about approaching Jesus. Leprosy was very contagious and also incurable, and most people didn't want lepers anywhere near them. In fact, people usually ran away when they saw a leper coming. But Jesus didn't. The poor man knelt before Him, his skin misshapen and ugly with sores, and said, "I know that you can cure me, if you want to."

"Of course I want to," Jesus murmured, and He reached out and placed His hand on the leper's crumbling skin.

It took a couple of moments for the leper

to recover from the shock. After all, most people wouldn't dream of touching him.

But then the man looked at his hands, his legs, and felt his face. His skin was healed. He was cured!

"Don't tell anyone," Jesus told the man, who was sobbing his gratitude. "Just go to your priest so he can see for himself and make an offering of thanks to God."

Another time, Jesus shocked many people when He helped an officer in the Roman army. After all, most Jewish people hated the Romans because they had taken control of Israel. The Roman officer begged Jesus to

253

help his servant who was lying ill at home in great pain. "I will come with you straight away," Jesus told the Roman officer.

"That won't be necessary," the Roman insisted. "I know if you just give the word for my servant to recover, he will do so."

Jesus was stunned and delighted. "I haven't met a Jewish person who has shown as much faith as this," He said. "There will be many people from far-off lands who will be able to enter the Kingdom of Heaven, while many from the nation of Israel will be locked outside."

The Roman officer returned home to find his servant completely cured.

Matthew chapter 8; Mark chapter 1; Luke chapter 7; John chapter 4

Jesus Befriends Outcasts

One day Jesus was walking down a street with many of his disciples. He peered through a window and saw a man called Matthew busy working at a desk in the tax office. Jesus thought how lonely he looked. He realized that Matthew must have very few friends, if any at all. He was working as a tax collector for the Romans who were ruling Israel, and Jewish people hated the Romans. They wanted them out of their country. Tax collectors were seen to be working for the enemy.

Jesus took pity on Matthew. "Come with me," He said, with a kind smile.

Matthew felt he simply had to do as he was told. He got up, leaving his work exactly as it was, and went off with Jesus and His followers.

After that, Matthew didn't want to lose his kind, new friend. When it grew late in the day, Matthew insisted that Jesus should be his guest for supper. He invited some of the other workers from the tax office too. His usually quiet little house was filled with the happy sound of people chatting over an enjoyable meal.

Of course, when the local Pharisees heard what was going on, they didn't like it one bit. "Jesus should be sitting down to eat with important, holy people like us," they grumbled, "not common folk—and shameful traitors too!"

But Jesus explained, "I haven't come to befriend only good people. In fact, it's sinners who need me the most."

Jesus once went to dinner at the house of a Pharisee, and He wasn't very impressed. The man, called Simon, didn't give him a warm welcome at all. It was good manners for a host to greet his guests with a kiss, and give them some perfume to refresh

themselves with. It was also usual for a host
to give guests some water and towels so
they (or a servant) could wash the dust off
their feet. Simon the Pharisee did none of
these things for Jesus.

However, during the meal,
a woman crept into the room
who had lived a very
sinful life. Other
people thought she was
shameful and wouldn't
have anything to do with
her. But now, the woman
knelt before Jesus and
begged for forgiveness,
sobbing quietly. Her falling tears wet Jesus'
feet, and she used her long hair to dry them.

Then she soothed them with some expensive perfume that she had brought.

"See," Jesus said to Simon the Pharisee, "you think of yourself as a holy man and this woman as sinful, but she has shown me every kindness that you have not. It doesn't matter at all that she has done wrong in the past, she is now truly sorry and her sins are all forgiven."

And the woman went home with joy in her heart, determined to follow Jesus and live a good life from then on.

Matthew chapter 9; Mark chapter 2; Luke chapters 5, 7

Jesus Calms
the Storm

Jesus had been preaching to a huge crowd
by the Sea of Galilee all day. Evening
began drawing in and He felt exhausted.
Jesus needed to escape the masses of people
and rest. "Let's sail to the other side of the
lake," He said to a few of his disciples. They
all climbed into a boat, pushed off from the

shore, and raised the sail.

Soon the little boat was speeding across the waters in the setting sun. Jesus sat back, his head drooped, and he nodded off, lulled to sleep by the rise and fall of the sea.

While Jesus lay dreaming, the disciples were alarmed to see black clouds overhead. The wind rose, stirring up the water. The disciples hurried to roll up the sail as the gale grew stronger. It whisked the waves up into great peaks, which sent the boat rearing up and then plunging down. Water crashed over the sides. Despite their efforts to bail out the water, the waves kept breaking in, threatening to sink the boat.

Amazingly Jesus slept through it all. But now the terrified disciples woke him.

"Master!" they shouted, struggling to make their voices heard over the wailing winds. "Master, we're all going to drown!"

Jesus opened his eyes and got to his feet. His hair and clothes whipped around him as he stretched out his hands, looked up to the skies and cried, "Be still!"

At once the wind dropped, the waves died away and the clouds faded. All was peaceful again.

But now the disciples were frightened for a new reason. What kind of man could command the wind and the waves?

Matthew chapter 8; Mark chapter 4; Luke chapter 8

Two Fish and Five Loaves

There came a time when the King of Judea had John the Baptist, Jesus' good friend, thrown into prison and put to death. When Jesus heard the news, He was preaching at the Sea of Galilee. He was upset and wanted to escape the crowds who followed Him everywhere, so He could be on His own for a little while. Jesus and His twelve disciples took a little boat out across the waters. However, the hundreds of people who had come to see and hear Jesus raced around the coast, joined by more people they met on the way. The crowd was there waiting for Jesus and His friends when they arrived on the far shore.

Jesus looked at the great mass of people—many of them sick or injured, hoping desperately for a cure. His heart went out to them. "Look at them," Jesus murmured. "They are like sheep without a shepherd."

Even though Jesus was grief-stricken and exhausted, He began preaching and healing… and was still talking to the people when dusk began to fall.

"Master, you've done enough now," the disciples said, concerned for Jesus. "It's time everyone went home. We all need something to eat."

Jesus smiled wearily. "No one needs to go anywhere," He said. "You can find us all some dinner."

The disciples looked at each other in confusion. They were surrounded by at least five thousand people. How did Jesus expect the disciples to feed them all?

"We've hardly any money between all of us to buy anything for supper," Philip pointed out.

Andrew added, "The only food we have is what this lad has brought with him," and he indicated a young boy carrying a basket. "He's got five loaves of bread and two fish, but they'll hardly go very far!"

Jesus stretched out his hands over the loaves and fish, said a blessing and broke them into pieces. Then He told his disciples, "Now share them out among everyone."

The disciples knew that they should trust Jesus, no matter what. To their amazement, there was enough bread and fish for everybody to have a hearty supper and enough left over to fill twelve baskets.

Matthew chapter 14; Mark chapter 6; Luke chapter 9; John chapter 6

Walking
on Water

It had been a long day at the Sea of
Galilee. Jesus told his weary disciples to
head for home without Him while He sent
away the thousands of people who had
gathered. "It's going to take a little while
for me to convince everyone to leave," Jesus
said to His friends with a sigh. "You start

off without me. I want to spend some time praying on my own. I'll catch up with you."

"But how will you follow us?" The disciples protested, clambering into their little boats.

"Don't worry, I'll be fine," Jesus reassured them, waving them off.

As the men sailed away, Jesus turned back to the crowds and told them it was time to go home too. No one wanted to leave Him, but eventually they began to wander away in groups. At last, Jesus was able to leave unnoticed and went a little way up a hillside. Finally, He had some peace and quiet and could pray alone. He stayed for quite a while, deep in thought, talking to God.

Meanwhile out on the Sea of Galilee, the disciples were in trouble. The wind had grown stronger, stirring up strong currents in the water and battering the little boats. The alarmed men rolled up the sails and tried to row to shore, but despite straining at the oars with all their might, the boats were being blown off course, out into dangerous open waters.

Hours passed and as the night grew darker, the wind grew wilder and the waves grew higher. The disciples realized they were lost at sea and they were terrified.

As they sat huddled in their boats, desperately waiting for the light of dawn,

they saw a white glow in the darkness. It
came closer and grew bigger,
turning into the shape of a
man. "A ghost!"
they cried, even
more frightened
than before.
Then a voice came
floating toward
them on the wind.

"Don't be afraid. It's me,
Jesus."

The disciples were confused.
Was it really their friend and
master? Or was a demon
trying to trick them?

Peter spoke up bravely.

"If it's really you, Lord," he shouted back, "tell me to walk to you across the waves."

"Yes, come then," Jesus called.

Peter stood up, cautiously moved to the edge of the rocking boat and took a deep breath. The other disciples could hardly believe their eyes as Peter stepped out.

Far from sinking into the churning waters, their friend strode from wave to wave, over the swirling sea, toward Jesus.

Peter kept his eyes fixed on Jesus, not daring to look down. But when he was within a couple of steps of Jesus, his curiosity got the better of him and he glanced down. The moment he saw the frothing foam beneath his feet, his courage deserted him and he plunged down into the dark, cold waters. "Help me, Jesus!" Peter screamed in a panic. "I'm sinking!"

Jesus reached out and grabbed Peter's hand, heaving him up. "Don't doubt me," He said. "Have more faith." Jesus guided his friend back to the boats and suddenly the wind died down and the waves calmed.

The disciples had watched everything in amazement. "You really are the Son of God," they said, falling in awe at Jesus' feet.

Matthew chapter 14; Mark chapter 6; John chapter 6

A Visit to Martha and Mary

Jesus once stopped in a little village called Bethany. A woman called Martha who lived in the village invited Jesus and His disciples into her house to rest and eat. They were grateful and accepted her kind offer.

Martha introduced the men to her sister, Mary. Then she showed Jesus and His

friends to where they could sit, and began
bustling about. First she disappeared into
the kitchen and brought out bowls of water
and towels so that they could freshen up
from the dust of the road. Then she went to
fetch pitchers of juice and drinking cups to
quench their thirst. Back to the kitchen she
dashed to prepare trays of hot drinks and
plates of food.

Meanwhile, Mary
had made herself
comfortable at
Jesus' feet. While
Martha was racing
about, seeing to
their guests, Mary
sat and gazed up at

the great preacher, listening intently to every word He said.

"Mary, it would be nice if you gave me a hand," Martha whispered, carrying another tray of food.

But her sister didn't follow her back to the kitchen. Instead, Martha found herself cooking dinner for thirteen guests all on her own. How fed up she felt! After all, she would like to be sitting and chatting with the famous preacher and His twelve friends. But somebody had to prepare the food, and her sister wasn't going to do it.

So Martha continued to make trips back and forth from the kitchen, carrying in starters, main courses, and desserts, and clearing away tray after tray of empty plates, bowls, and cups.

By the time everyone had finished eating
and Martha had cleared everything away,
Jesus, the disciples, and Mary were deep in
conversation. Martha had missed the start
of the discussion so she couldn't really
understand what they were talking about.
And her guests had all spread out so much
in the room that there was hardly space for
her to sit down.

How left out Martha felt! As she looked
at her sister sitting right next to Jesus,
having done nothing at all, she felt a lump
rise in her throat and tears begin to prick
her eyes.

"Lord," she suddenly burst out in
frustration, "how could you let my sister just

sit there lazily and do nothing? Why didn't you tell her to get up and help?"

"My poor Martha, thank you so much for your kindness," Jesus said, getting up to comfort the upset woman. "But you have prepared so many different dishes for us when just one would have been enough. Your sister has chosen to pay attention to me in the best way of all—listening. I can't possibly tell her off for that."

Luke chapter 10

Lazarus
is Awoken

Amessenger brought urgent news to
Jesus from Martha and Mary, the two
women he had stayed with in the village of
Bethany. Their brother, Lazarus, had fallen
seriously ill and they feared he was dying.

Jesus had made firm friends with the two
sisters and their brother, and was fond of

them. But to the disciples' surprise He didn't rush off when He received the message. "Lazarus will be fine," Jesus told them. "God has made him ill on purpose in order to show His glorious power through me."

Jesus stayed where He was, preaching and healing for another two days. On the third day He told the disciples that He was at last heading back to Bethany. "I have to wake Lazarus," He explained.

"But master," protested the disciples, rather puzzled, "if Lazarus is sleeping, won't he wake up on his own?"

"Lazarus is dead," Jesus announced calmly. "And I am glad I wasn't there to save him because now I can work a miracle that will give you more faith in me."

By the time Jesus arrived at Bethany Lazarus had been dead for four days. As he approached the sisters' house, a red-eyed Martha came out. "Oh Lord," she sobbed, "if only you had been here, Lazarus would not have died." Wiping her tears, she looked at Jesus. "But I know that God will grant you anything you ask for," she whispered.

Jesus was moved by Martha's faith. Holding her gaze, He asked, "Do you accept that anyone who believes in me and dies will live again? That anyone who believes in me and lives will never die?"

"I do, my Lord," replied Martha.

"Then fetch your sister and show me where you have buried your brother," Jesus said gently.

Martha hurried to fetch Mary, and together they and their grief-stricken friends accompanied Jesus to Lazarus' tomb. He had been laid to rest in a cave with a large stone set across the entrance.

"Roll away the rock," Jesus ordered.

The sisters were shocked. "But master, he has been dead for four days," said Martha. "His body will smell."

Jesus waved away their protests. As everyone helped clear the entrance, He started to pray. "Father, you always hear me and answer me," Jesus said, "and I thank you with all my heart. Now I am asking for something that will help everyone believe that it's you who have sent me."

Jesus shut his eyes and stood very still.

Then his firm, clear voice echoed into the cave. "Lazarus, come out!" He commanded.

After a while, everyone heard a shuffling sound and a shrouded figure came staggering out of the cave.

"Don't be afraid, unwrap your brother," Jesus urged Mary and Martha.

Hardly daring to breathe, they did so. Lazarus was alive and well again.

John chapters 11 to 27

283

Bartimaeus, the Blind Beggar

Bartimaeus had been a blind beggar in Jericho for as long as anyone could remember. No one knew how old he was, probably not even Bartimaeus himself, but everyone knew who he was. He could always be found sitting in the same spot by the roadside. His begging bowl set on the ground in front of him, and lifting his poor, dull eyes hopefully to each passerby.

One day Bartimaeus became aware of quite a fuss building around him. "What's going on?" he asked. "Why are there so many people around?"

"Jesus of Nazareth is coming this way," someone replied.

At once, Bartimaeus' heart began to beat faster. He had heard many stories about the great preacher—how He had given the gift of sight to hundreds of blind people just like him. Jesus had healed paralyzed people, cured the lame, made the sick well again. It was rumored that Jesus had even brought people back from the dead.

As the crowds bustled around the beggar,

he stumbled to his feet and added his voice to theirs. "Jesus! Have pity on me!" he shouted as loud as he could.

"Be quiet, Bartimaeus! Shut up!" came voices from around him. "Jesus is coming and we want to hear what he is saying."

But that just encouraged Bartimaeus to shout even louder. "Jesus of Nazareth! Help me!" he bellowed, with a strength he didn't know he had. "I'm over here. Please take pity on me!"

Suddenly, the commotion all around him fell silent and he felt a hand on his shoulder.

"My friend, I'm here," came a soft voice. "How would you like me to help you?"

Trembling, Bartimaeus gasped, "Oh Lord, please let me see."

The man felt gentle fingertips touch his eyelids. Then all at once the darkness before him began to lighten and brighten until he could make out blurs... then shapes and colors... He could see! The world was unimaginably beautiful, and Bartimaeus looked at Jesus' smiling face.

"Your faith has made you well," Jesus said, and Bartimaeus followed Him, dancing in celebration along the road.

Matthew chapter 20; Mark chapter 10; Luke chapter 18

Jesus Teaches through Stories

Jesus often preached about God and the way to happiness in Heaven by telling people stories with hidden meanings, called parables. He once told a parable about a farmer who was sowing seed in his field. As he went, he scattered seed all around him so it would grow.

"Some of the seed fell onto the footpath," said Jesus, "so it didn't sink into the soil and birds swooped down and ate it up. These seeds never had a chance to grow."

Jesus went on, "Other seeds fell onto rocky, stony ground. They started to grow, but couldn't put down deep, strong roots. Under the hot summer sun, the young crops couldn't take up enough moisture from the earth and they withered, scorched, and died."

Jesus continued, "Some seeds landed on patches of thorny weeds. The crops grew but the weeds grew up faster and choked

them. However, some
seeds fell onto good,
rich soil and they
grew into tall,
plentiful crops."
Jesus didn't tell His listeners
what the parable meant. He
wanted them to try to understand
it for themselves. That way, they would
really think about what Jesus had told them
and they wouldn't forget His message.

Later Jesus explained to His disciples.
"The seed is the Word of God. The footpath
stands for people who hear the Word of
God but who don't take it in. The devil will
swoop down and seize it from them so they
forget. The seed that falls on rocky ground

stands for people who listen to the Word of God but don't take it in. When they are faced with problems, their difficulties overcome them. The seed that falls among weeds stands for people who hear the Word of God but get distracted by selfish habits and desires. Finally, the seed that falls onto good soil stands for people who take the Word of God into their hearts. Over time it grows there and bears fruit."

Jesus warned everyone to listen hard to His parables. "No one buys a lamp and hides its light," he said. "So don't ignore my teachings. Everything I am telling you will one day prove to be true."

Matthew chapter 13; Mark chapter 4; Luke chapter 8

A Story of Forgiveness

Jesus told a story about a farmer who had two sons. The farmer was teaching his sons all about farming so that when he died, they could take over. However one day, the younger son approached his father with an idea.

"I've been thinking, father," he said

nervously. "I'm grown up and it's time I saw a bit of the world. It would help if I could have my share of the farm now in cash."

The farmer loved his sons dearly and he didn't even have to think about the decision. He counted hundreds of silver coins into bags and handed them to the excited lad.

"Thank you, father," he said, packing his bags to set off. "You won't regret it."

And the farmer watched with tears in his eyes as his younger son left home.

For a while the farmer's son had a wonderful time. He lived like a prince, visiting the finest cities, eating out every night, and going to parties. He was surrounded by people who wanted to be his friend, but the problem was they helped him spend all his money. When the silver was gone, his friends vanished too. The young man found himself alone and far from home, without even a few pennies to buy a loaf of bread. To make matters worse, a dreadful drought swept through the land, causing a terrible famine. The farmer's son couldn't even beg for food because no one had enough for themselves. Luckily, he found a job as a pig-keeper. But the wages were pitiful. He had hardly enough money left to buy food after paying his rent. Some days he was so hungry he nearly ate the food for the pigs!

One day, he decided enough was enough. "I want to go home," he groaned. "I'll beg my father for his forgiveness for being such an idiot. He's bound to be furious, but maybe if I grovel, he'll let me stay and work as one of his farm laborers."

The miserable, ragged young man arrived home and couldn't believe how overjoyed his father was to see him. "I've worried about you and missed you every day, son," the farmer cried, hugging and kissing him. The ashamed son sobbed as he told his father what had happened.

"Never mind," the farmer said, to his

son's utter astonishment. "You're back home now and we're together again. That's all that matters."

Later, the farmer's elder son came home from a hard day's work in the fields to find a party in full swing. The neighbors had been invited over to celebrate, and a feast had been prepared. There was music, dancing, and the people were drinking wine.

"Whatever's going on here?" he gasped, and one of the servants explained what had happened.

The farmer swung his elder son round in a jig. "Rejoice!" he cried. "Your little brother has finally come back home!"

"What do you mean, rejoice?" the elder

son spat, completely furious. "I've stayed with you all these years, working my fingers to the bone, and you've never given me so much as a thank you—let alone thrown me a party! Then HE turns up, having wasted most of your fortune, and you're celebrating how wonderful he is!"

"You have no idea how much your faithfulness means to me," the farmer said to his elder son, drawing him close in a hug. "Everything I have, I give to you. But today is a day to be glad, for your brother was lost and gone forever, but he has come home."

Luke chapter 15

The Pharisee and the Tax Collector

The Pharisees were Jews who had been brought up to live according to strict religious rules. They believed that their ways of living were the right ways—the only ways—and everyone who didn't follow their rules was not as good as them.

However, Jesus often warned the

Pharisees that they were committing all sorts of sins without realizing it. One was the sin of looking down on others, and He told this story to try to make the Pharisees think about it.

"Two men went into the temple to pray. One was a Pharisee," the Pharisees in the crowd of listeners all smiled smugly, "and one was a tax collector," people booed and hissed at the thought of the traitors who worked for the Romans. "The Pharisee strode straight into the middle of the temple," Jesus continued, "in full view of the people around. He lifted his arms, raised his eyes to the heavens, and prayed in a loud, confident voice so that everyone could clearly hear him. 'Thank you, O God,' he said, 'for making me better than common sinners. Thank you for not making me a liar or a cheat like most people. Thank you for giving me the strength to fast twice a week and the generosity to give part of everything I earn to charity. Thank you for not making me like that greedy tax collector over there.'

"The tax collector was lurking behind a pillar in the shadows, trying his best not to be noticed by anyone. He knelt and bowed his head low, whispering, 'Lord, I am a sinner. I ask for forgiveness, even though I am not worthy of your mercy.'

"Now," finished Jesus, "That day it was the tax collector who went home with God's blessing. For those who set themselves up high will one day fall, and those who think of themselves as lowly will one day be raised up."

Of course the Pharisees didn't like that particular story one little bit.

Luke chapter 18

The Parable of the Lost Coins

Despite everything Jesus had told His followers, there were many people who thought that He was going to establish God's Kingdom by forming an army and marching against the Romans. Jesus knew that He wasn't going to win any earthly revolution. In fact, He was going to be

arrested, put on trial, and then executed.
The Kingdom of Heaven would come at
the end of the world, after Judgment Day,
and only God knew when that would be.
So Jesus told a parable that he hoped would
help people make the most of everything
God had given them, while they were
waiting.

"There was once a prince who had to
travel far away to lay claim to a kingdom
that was rightfully his," Jesus began.
"Before he went, he called his three most
trusted servants and asked them to look
after his property while he was away. To the
first servant he gave five bags of gold. To
the second servant he gave two bags and to
the third servant he gave one bag. 'Use my

money wisely and well,' he bade them.

"The prince left and years passed. Eventually he returned, now a great king. 'What did you do with my gold,' he asked his servants.

"The first servant traded with his five bags of gold and earned five more. The king was delighted and made him governor of ten of his new cities.

"The second servant had saved his two bags of gold in a bank, where it had doubled with interest making four bags. The king was pleased and made

him governor of five new cities.

"The last servant had hidden his bag of gold in the ground. 'You mean to say you did nothing with my gift?' the king roared furiously. 'You made no use of it at all?' He turned to his guards. 'Take this man's gold and then throw him out,' he commanded. 'Give the gold to the servant who already has ten bags. For those who try hard will be rewarded, while those who do not will lose what little they have.'

Matthew chapter 25; Luke chapter 19

The Good Samaritan

Jesus always surprised people by knowing Jewish religious rules inside out and back to front. Many religious leaders and holy men who had spent their whole lives studying the laws were jealous of Jesus' knowledge. So they would ask tricky questions to try to catch Him out.

One day a lawyer came to Jesus and asked, "What must I do to win eternal life?"

"What does the law tell you to do?" Jesus answered simply.

"To love God with all my heart and soul, and to love my neighbor as I love myself," the lawyer reeled off smugly, showing off his knowledge.

"Exactly," said Jesus. "If you already know, why are you asking me?"

"Ah, but who is my neighbor?" the man asked, feeling confident that he had posed a question far too difficult for Jesus to answer.

"Let me tell you a story," Jesus said, without a moment's hesitation. "There was once a man traveling on the road from Jerusalem to Jericho. Suddenly a group of

bandits sprang out from behind some rocks
and attacked him. There was no one
around to hear the
traveler's cries for
help. The bandits
beat him, robbed
him of all his
possessions, and left
him for dead.

"After a while, a
priest came walking down
the road," Jesus continued. "He wondered
what a bundle of rags was doing in the
middle of the road and went over to have a
look. As soon as the priest saw that the heap
was actually a man lying bleeding in the
dust, he quickly crossed to the other side of

the road. He didn't want to know what had happened or have anything to do with it."

The lawyer gasped, "How could such a holy man not help someone in need?"

"The next traveler to approach was a Levite," Jesus carried on.

"This man is sure to help," said the Lawyer. Jews from the tribe of Levi were so god-fearing that priests were always chosen from among them.

"The Levite shuddered in disgust when he saw the battered and bruised man barely alive," Jesus continued. "Like the priest

309

before him, he crossed to the far side of the road and walked away."

Now the lawyer was really shocked. A holy Levite should have known better.

"Next, a Samaritan passed by," Jesus announced.

The lawyer pulled a face. Samaritans were the people who had been sent to live in Israel when the Jews were taken away as slaves by the Babylonians. The Jews hated the Samaritans for taking their land. They also looked down on the Samaritans because they weren't God's Chosen People and often didn't worship God at all. The lawyer thought the Samaritan probably went over to see if there was anything left to steal!

But Jesus continued, "The Samaritan was appalled when he saw the injured man and rushed to help. He gave the poor man some water, heaved him up onto his donkey, and hurried to the nearest town. There he paid an innkeeper to take him in and look after him until he was better."

The lawyer was flabbergasted.

"Now which of the three travelers would you say was the neighbor of the attacked man?" Jesus asked.

"The one who helped him," stuttered the lawyer.

"Right," said Jesus. "Now go and behave like the Samaritan."

Luke chapter 10

Jesus and the Children

The twelve disciples were traveling with Jesus along a road one day. They began to fall behind, squabbling among themselves. Their argument was about which of them would be the greatest in the Kingdom of Heaven. They thought that Jesus couldn't hear them, but He did. They were saying things like, "Well, I should be the greatest because I'm Jesus' oldest friend…" And, "I should be the greatest because I've performed the most miracles…" And, "No, I'm sure I'll be the greatest because I pray the most often."

Jesus didn't stop them, He just listened to every word. But later on when they had reached their destination and sat down to rest, He asked, "So what were you all talking about on the road then?"

The disciples felt embarrassed to think that Jesus had heard them trying to outdo each other. No one admitted a thing, but Jesus knew all about what had gone on. "If you really want to be the greatest in God's eyes, you must put others before yourself,"

He told the red-faced men. Jesus reached out to a little girl who was passing by and drew her toward Him. "You must be like this child," He said. "You must have simple, honest values and take genuine delight in helping others. Never look down on children, for they are selfless and giving. They are among the greatest in Heaven."

However, it didn't take long for the disciples to forget what Jesus had told them. A few weeks later, Jesus had been preaching all day long when a group of people with young children approached, asking Him to bless them. Some of the children clung to their parents, while others were playful and pestered Jesus for attention. Jesus' disciples were sure that this would be annoying for the weary preacher and they began to shoo the children away. But Jesus stopped his friends. "Let the children come to me," He instructed. "After all, the Kingdom of Heaven belongs to them." Jesus picked up the smallest child and let others scramble onto his lap, blessing them all. "Unless you are pure and wholehearted like these children," He warned his disciples once more, "you will never see God."

Matthew chapters 18, 19; Mark chapters 9, 10;
Luke chapters 9, 18

Jesus the Good Shepherd

Jesus once said to a crowd that had gathered to hear him speak, "What would a shepherd do if wolves attacked the sheep in his flock? If he was a hired shepherd, doing his job only for the money, he wouldn't stay and fight off the wolves. He would run away and save himself, leaving the sheep to be eaten. I am not like that shepherd, I am the good shepherd. I will look after my sheep even if it means I have to die for them. I have flocks in other places too, which I need to gather so I can look after all my animals together. My sheep know my voice, they will listen to me and follow me anywhere. It's because I will give up my life for my sheep willingly—for love, not any other reward—that God loves me and will give me my life back again."

Many of Jesus' listeners were puzzled by these words. "He must be mad," some of them mumbled. "Do you think it's demons inside Him that are talking?"

But others knew that Jesus was trying to get them to understand something important. "Of course He's not mad!" they insisted, even though they weren't sure what Jesus meant. "How could someone possessed by demons miraculously heal people?" What Jesus wanted everyone to know was that He genuinely cared for them. Not just for Jewish people, but for people everywhere who wanted to follow God. He was also warning that He was ready to die for everybody, if that is what He had to do. Jesus was explaining that it is only by loving everyone and willingly helping other people in this world, that God will reward us with new life in the next.

John chapter 10

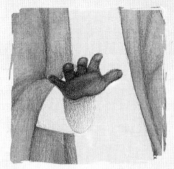

Jesus Warns
of the Future

There came a rare moment when Jesus
found Himself alone with His disciples,
walking along a road. He took the
opportunity to talk with them. "I sometimes
call myself 'the Son of Man'," He began.
"What do you think I mean by that?"

"Some people believe you are John the

Baptist," one disciple shrugged.

"Or the prophet Elijah come back from the dead," another suggested.

"Or a new, greater prophet," a third said.

"But who do you think I am?" He asked.

"I think you are the Messiah, the Son of the Living God," Peter announced firmly.

"Then God has blessed you," Jesus said to Peter. "Your name means rock, and you are the rock on which I will build my church. I will give you the keys to Heaven, and whatever rules you set on Earth will also stand in Heaven."

Jesus turned to everyone and said gravely, "I must warn you

all that things are soon going to get very difficult. The time is drawing near when I must go to Jerusalem. I will go through much suffering," Jesus gave a sigh. "And eventually I will be put to death." The disciples gasped, but Jesus held up his hands to silence them. "However, three days later, I will come back to life."

The disciples were amazed.

"Are you ready to follow me into hardship and sorrow—even to die for me?" Jesus asked his friends. "If you are, I cannot grant you a reward in this world, but I can promise you joy in the next."

Jesus' friends walked on with heavy, but determined, hearts.

Matthew chapter 16; Mark chapter 8; Luke chapter 9

Jesus Shows Himself in Glory

One week had passed since Jesus told his disciples that He was the Messiah and warned them of the troubles to come. Now He asked Peter, James, and John to go with Him up a hillside a little way to a quiet place where they could pray away from everyone else.

The four men were soon deep in prayer, unaware of anything else around them. But suddenly something made Peter, James, and John stop talking to God and turn to look at Jesus. They were shocked to see their kneeling friend so transfixed in prayer. His body looked still and lifeless like a statue, as if His spirit had left it. Jesus' face began to glow brighter and brighter, and His clothes glared whiter and whiter, until He was surrounded by a blaze of glory. It hurt their eyes to look at Him, so they shielded them with their hands.

Two other gleaming figures appeared whom they recognized as the great prophets, Moses and Elijah. They listened as Jesus discussed with them what He would have to face in Jerusalem, including His own death.

Then suddenly a towering black cloud surged overhead. "This is my Son, the Chosen One. Listen to Him!" boomed a mighty voice. The disciples were terrified.

When they looked up again, everything had returned to normal. "Don't tell anyone what you have seen," Jesus commanded, "until I have died and risen from the dead."

Matthew chapter 17; Mark chapter 9; Luke chapter 9

The First
Palm Sunday

It was the week before the great feast of
Passover. Jews from far-off lands traveled
to Jerusalem for the celebrations, which
lasted several days. Jewish holy men such as
the chief priests and Pharisees were waiting
to see if Jesus would dare visit the city too.
They had been plotting for a long time to

arrest and execute the preacher who they thought was stirring up the people and leading them astray. The Jewish leaders thought Jesus might enter Jerusalem unnoticed by mingling among the crowds, so they sent spies through Jerusalem to see if they could spot Him.

However Jesus was planning to arrive quite openly. When He and His disciples were a little way off, on the Mount of Olives, Jesus sent two of His friends into the village of Bethphage to find a donkey for him to ride. "You will find one tethered to a doorway," He told them. "Untie it and bring it to me. If anyone objects, just explain that it's me who needs it and they won't stop you."

The disciples found the donkey, just as He had said. When the owners heard who wanted it, they brought it to Jesus themselves. They even threw their cloaks onto its back to make a comfortable saddle for Him to sit on. The little animal had never been ridden before, but it stood calm and willing as Jesus climbed onto it.

Jesus patted the donkey's head, then set off for the city of Jerusalem. When people along the way saw Him coming, they cheered, sang, and danced for joy. The ancient prophets had said that the Messiah would ride into Jerusalem on a donkey. And so the people realized that Jesus was claiming openly for the first time that He was the savior they had been waiting for.

"Hosanna!" they shouted, lining the donkey's path with their cloaks and palm leaves. "Blessed is He who comes in the name of the Lord! Hosanna in the highest!"

People jammed the streets to welcome Jesus all the way into Jerusalem.

"This is outrageous!" the furious Pharisees bellowed at Jesus. "You're making these people think you're the Messiah!"

"Even if they were quiet," Jesus replied, "the stones themselves would cry out to greet me."

Matthew chapter 21; Mark chapter 11; Luke chapter 19; John chapters 11, 12

Jesus and the Temple Traders

As all good Jews did at the feast of Passover, Jesus went to pray at the great temple. He expected to see the courtyards filled with respectful worshipers deep in prayer, moving quietly about so as not to disturb others. Instead, Jesus was horrified to find the sacred building being used as a marketplace.

Everywhere He looked, there were
stallholders selling doves and other animals
for sacrifices. They cried out their wares,
competing for business. People bartered
with them, trying to get the best prices,
while doves cooed and lambs bleated.
Among the stalls were money-changers,
haggling with worshipers and counting out
foreign money into Jewish shekels. All the
traders were charging unfair prices,
and the worshipers had no choice but to
pay. Everyone had to offer a sacrifice and
give shekels to the temple funds at Passover.
Meanwhile, city traders were using the
temple courtyards and corridors to get from
one side of Jerusalem to another.

As Jesus stood amid the hubbub, he grew furious. Suddenly, He began sending the traders' tables flying into the air, kicking down stalls, smashing dove cages open, and ripping animal tethers loose. "This is the house of God, but you have turned it into a robbers' den!" He yelled, clearing the temple of everyone except for genuine worshipers.

It wasn't long before the courtyards were full again. This time, with people who had come to hear Jesus preach.

Matthew chapter 21; Luke chapter 19

Jesus Against the Authorities

Every day of Passover week Jesus stood in the temple preaching to huge crowds and healing many people too. The Jewish leaders were enraged. "Who gives you the right to say and do these things?" they demanded. "Listen to what the people are saying about you—they think you are the Messiah! We are warning you to stop." They sent holy men such as the Pharisees and Sadducees to try to make Jesus break the law in some way so they could arrest Him. But Jesus waged a war of words on them and won every time.

"Holy men such as the Pharisees say that you should follow the rules of Moses," He told everyone one day. "This is right, so listen to what they say. But don't do as they do because they don't practice what they preach!"

People in the crowd began to argue angrily with each other—the Jewish leaders and their followers on one side, and Jesus and His disciples on the other.

Jesus continued, "Everything the holy

men do is for show. They say aloud long prayers in public so everyone can admire them. They wear fancy robes so they stand out in the crowd. They sit at the front at the synagogue and expect to be addressed as "Teacher." But I say you have only one teacher—your Father in Heaven, and under Him, everyone is equal. Anyone who thinks they are better than others will one day find themselves the lowest. And anyone who serves others will one day find themselves the greatest."

Jesus criticized the Jewish elders in many other ways, leaving the people in uproar as they debated whether He was right or wrong. "Look at that lady over there," Jesus tried to explain. He pointed to a tiny, bent-over old woman in tatty clothes, shuffling to the temple collection box. With gnarled, trembling fingers, she dropped in a couple of copper coins and prayed. "That old woman is better than all the Jewish leaders," Jesus announced. "They only give what they can afford to charity, leaving plenty for themselves. This woman has hardly anything, but she has still given to God."

The Jewish leaders were determined to somehow seize Jesus. Every day He was surrounded by people in the temple. And every night He stayed outside the city, at Bethany. Jesus was safe for now.

Matthew chapters 21, 23; Mark chapter 12; Luke chapters 19, 21

The Last Supper

The Jewish leaders were extremely frustrated at their failure to get rid of Jesus. One night they gathered at the house of the chief priest, Caiaphas, for an emergency meeting. They were in the middle of discussing what they could do next when there was a knock at the door.

A servant ushered in a most unexpected guest. It was Judas Iscariot, one of Jesus' twelve disciples and closest friends.

"I'm here because I can give you what you want," he said, his eyes glinting coldly. "Jesus of Nazareth—how much is He worth to you?"

The Jewish officials didn't know what had made Judas become a traitor—and they didn't care either. They could hardly believe their good luck. They put their heads together for a few moments and then announced, "Thirty pieces of silver."

Without a word, Judas held out his hand and Caiaphas counted out the coins. From then on, Judas stayed by Jesus' side, waiting for the opportunity to betray Him.

Mysteriously, Jesus knew everything. With a heavy heart, He prepared for one last meal with his disciples—the Passover supper. He organized a room in secret, so that the Jewish leaders would not find out where He was, and only told His twelve friends about it at the last minute.

The disciples were in a very serious mood as they gathered together. After all, Jesus had warned them two days earlier that He was about to fall into the hands of His enemies and be put to death. As everything Jesus said came true, they were extremely worried.

While they settled at the table, Jesus wrapped a towel around his waist and filled a bowl with water. The disciples were

shocked to realize He was going to wash
the dust from their feet—a job usually done
by the very lowliest servant. Peter was
especially shocked and tried to stop Jesus
kneeling before him, but Jesus insisted. "I
am setting you all an example," Jesus said
afterward. "Always put others before
yourself."

Then it was time for dinner. Jesus took a
loaf of bread and asked for God's blessing
over it. "This is my body," He said with
great sadness, "which will be given up for
you." He broke the bread and gave it to all
the disciples to eat. Then Jesus poured a cup
of wine and asked for God's blessing over
that too. "This is my blood," He announced
gravely, "the sign of a new promise from

God. My blood will be spilt so that everyone's sins will be forgiven." One by one, the disciples took the cup and drank.

Then Jesus gestured for everyone to begin sharing out the different dishes on the table. As they did so, He gave a deep sigh.

"I know that one of you will betray me," He said softly. Cries of protest came up from around the table, but Jesus refused to explain further. As the disciples reluctantly turned back to eating, Peter murmured to John, who was sitting closest to Jesus, "Ask Him which of us He means."

John leaned over and spoke in Jesus' ear.

He whispered back, "The one to whom I will give this piece of bread."

John told Peter, and they watched as Jesus tore some bread and offered it to Judas Iscariot. "Do whatever you have to," Jesus told His disloyal friend, "but do it quickly."

And without a word Judas got up from the table and left the room.

Matthew chapter 26; Mark chapter 14; Luke chapter 22; John chapter 13

The Garden
of Gethsemane

After Jesus had shared His last supper
with the disciples, He sat back and
looked around at His dear friends. "I give
you a new commandment," He said. "Love
each other as I have loved you. By doing
this, everyone will know that you are my
followers."

"Lord, you've been talking all night as if you're leaving us," Peter protested.

"Yes," Jesus said gently. "I am going away, and where I am going you won't be able to follow me—for a while, at least."

"Why can't I follow you now?" Peter cried out. "I am ready to die for you!"

But Jesus smiled sadly. "Are you really, my friend?" He asked. "By the time this night is out and the rooster has crowed three times at dawn, you will have denied three times that you even know me."

"Never," Peter said, choking with sorrow. "Never." And all the disciples agreed strongly.

"Don't be upset," Jesus tried to comfort them. "I am going to prepare a place for you in my Father's house. And I will return to you for a short while, before I have to go away again for good. Even then when you will no longer be able to see me, I will always live in your hearts. Later, when the time is right, you will follow and we will be together again. Until then, do what I have done tonight as a way of remembering me. Be at peace, and be happy for me that I am going to be with my Father."

Jesus looked around at His friends' gloomy faces.

"Now come," He said gently. "Let's go to the Mount of Olives. I would like to pray in the Garden of Gethsemane for a while."

As they walked through the moonlight together, Jesus gave the disciples many more important instructions. He knew He only had a short time left in which to talk to them. When they finally reached the entrance to the Garden of Gethsemane, Jesus saw that the anxious men were exhausted. "Rest here while I go and pray," He told most of them. But He turned to Peter, James, and John and said, "I know you are tired, but would you come with me?"

The three were only too pleased to keep Jesus company. They had never seen Him look so strained and troubled before.

"My heart feels like it's breaking," Jesus sighed heavily when they had gone a little way. "Will you stay while I pray?"

Peter, James, and John watched as Jesus sank to his knees, His head in His hands.

"Father!" He cried
silently. Jesus prayed
that perhaps He might
not have to face the suffering
He knew lay ahead.

After a long while, Jesus
turned to Peter, James, and
John but saw they were asleep.
So Jesus prayed again. He felt the sins of
all the world weighing on His shoulders and
He knew the full horror of what was to
come.

Once more Jesus turned to his friends,
but they were still asleep.

And Jesus prayed again, willingly
accepting the suffering He had to face, so

that all people could one day reach God.

At last Jesus finished praying. Peter, James, and John were still asleep. But at that moment Judas Iscariot arrived, accompanied by a band of guards. At the noise of guards' swords and chains and the light from their flaming torches, the disciples woke up, startled. "Master," Judas said calmly, greeting Jesus with his usual kiss.

At that pre-arranged sign, the guards grabbed Jesus. After a brief commotion and panic, the disciples fled for their lives into the darkness.

Matthew chapter 26; Mark chapter 14; Luke chapter 22; John chapters 13, 14, 18

Peter
Denies Jesus

Surrounded by soldiers with weapons at the ready, that night Jesus was marched into the city of Jerusalem. Behind them, stumbling through the shadows went Peter, not letting his friend out of his sight for a second. He even followed when they reached the great house of the high priest,

Caiaphas. The guards marched Jesus into the front courtyard. But then the big doors opened, Jesus was hauled inside, and they banged shut. Peter could go no further.

How helpless Peter felt now! He had a sword with him in the Garden of Gethsemane, and slashing wildly he had managed to injure one of the guards, cutting off his ear. But Jesus shouted at him to stop, saying that violence was wrong. Jesus touched the soldier's ear and it had been instantly healed. Now Peter could do nothing except wait to see what happened.

Keeping his head down, Peter edged into a small group of servants and maids stood around a bonfire nearby. He sat quietly, trying not to draw attention to himself, wondering what terrors Jesus was facing.

"I know you," came a voice. Peter ignored it but the voice spoke again. "You're friends with the prisoner, Jesus of Galilee." It was a serving girl and she was pointing right at him.

"No I wasn't," Peter said, his heart suddenly racing. "You must have me confused with someone else."

"Yes, you were. I've seen you with him too," said another maid. And everyone stared at Peter and began mumbling to each other.

"I don't know him, I tell you," Peter said, his voice rising louder than he intended.

"You must be a follower of Jesus of Nazareth," accused a man right beside him.

"After all, you speak with the same accent as Him."

"I said I don't know anyone of that name!" Peter yelled, and he strode away. As he did so dawn began to break and the sound of a rooster crowing ripped through the air— once… twice… three times. Peter's head span as he remembered Jesus' words. "By the time this night is out and the rooster has crowed three times at dawn, you will have denied three times that you even know me." Sobbing with shame, loss, and fear, Peter ran away.

Matthew chapter 26; Mark chapter 14;
Luke chapter 22; John chapter 18

Jesus
on Trial

I nside Caiaphas' mansion, Jesus was quizzed by Annas, the former high priest. What did He think about ancient holy writings? What miracles did He claim to have worked? Who did He think He was?

Jesus refused to answer and was marched to a room full of Jewish officials. They had

witnesses who they had paid to lie, accusing
Jesus of saying and doing things that were
against Jewish law. But the witnesses
couldn't get their stories straight!

Finally Caiaphas hissed, "I order you to
tell us, under solemn oath, whether you
think you are the Son of God."

"I am," He said with grace, "and one
day you will see the Son of Man seated at
the right hand of the Father in Heaven."

"Blasphemy!" roared Caiaphas, a
satisfied gleam in his eyes. Blasphemy was
the crime of lying against God for which
the punishment was death.

In triumph, the Jewish elders had Jesus
blindfolded. They slapped and kicked Him,
shouting, "Prophesy for us now, Messiah.

Guess who hit you!" And in the morning, they had Jesus brought in front of the Roman governor, Pontius Pilate. Only he could approve an execution.

The news spread around the city and an enormous crowd gathered outside.

Pilate asked Jesus many more questions. Are you really a king? Have you been plotting against the Roman government? Have you been planning a rebellion?

Perplexed, Pilate couldn't find that Jesus had done anything wrong. He ordered that Jesus also be questioned by Herod, the ruler of Galilee, who was in Jerusalem at that time. But Herod couldn't find Jesus guilty of anything either. Even Pilate's wife told him that she had had a dream in which Jesus of

Nazareth was innocent of all charges. "Have nothing further to do with him," she advised her husband.

Pilate made his decision. He went out onto the balcony of his judgment hall and announced to the waiting crowds, "This man has done nothing to deserve death. He shall be whipped and let go." And Jesus was dragged off for His punishment.

Meanwhile the Jewish officials had

mingled with the crowds, persuading them that Jesus was guilty of blasphemy. As Pilate turned to go back into his Judgment Hall, people sent up cries of, "Kill him! Kill Jesus of Nazareth!"

The Roman governor was deeply disturbed, but he did not know what for. Suddenly he had an idea. Pilate remembered that it was Passover and there was a custom for the governor to release one prisoner of the people's choice. In the cells was a murderer called Barabbas. Pilate felt sure that the people would rather have Jesus released than a violent killer.

"Who shall I pardon—Barabbas or Jesus of Nazareth?" Pilate asked the crowd.

He couldn't believe his ears when the

shouts came back, "Barabbas!"

Pilate ordered that Jesus be brought in front of him once more. He had been whipped until blood poured down His back. The guards had mocked him as the King of the Jews, too, by pressing a crown of thorns onto His head and throwing a cloak around his shoulders.

Now the crowd jeered too.

Pilate had had enough. He called for water and a towel, and washed his hands in front of everyone. "I cleanse myself of this man's blood," he announced.

Then Barabbas was released and Jesus was led away to be crucified.

Matthew chapters 26, 27; Mark chapters 14, 15;
Luke chapters 22, 23; John chapters 18, 19

The Crucifixion

Jesus had withstood being marched about in chains, hours of angry questioning, a beating from the Jewish officials, and being brutally whipped by Pilate's guards. The crown of thorns was still pressed into His head, sending blood trickling down His pain-filled face.

Two Roman soldiers lifted a huge, solid wooden cross over Jesus' shoulder—so heavy that He nearly collapsed from the weight of it. Then Jesus staggered onward, through the streets of Jerusalem and toward the hill outside the city where He and two other criminals were to be executed.

Thousands of people lined the way, watching the procession. Jesus willed Himself forward, heavy step after heavy step. But eventually He crashed into the dust, utterly exhausted. The angry guards dragged a strong man from the crowd called Simon of Cyrene and ordered him to carry the cross instead.

People in the crowd yelled insults and spat on Jesus as He stumbled by. But Jesus caught sight of the sorrowful faces of many friends He had made too. Many of the women were weeping. "Don't cry for me," Jesus said, "but for yourselves, your children, and for the destruction that is to come."

Eventually they reached the place for the execution. It was called Golgotha, meaning "place of the skull." A soldier made Jesus lie down on the cross, and long nails were hammered into His hands and feet. "Father forgive them, for they don't know what they are doing," Jesus moaned. A notice was fixed above his head which said "Jesus of Nazareth, King of the Jews" in three languages. "It shouldn't say that," some Jewish officials objected. "It should say 'This man said he was the King of the Jews'."

But the Roman governor, Pilate, boomed, "I ordered it to be written just like that and that is the way it will stay!"

The Jewish officials mocked as Jesus' cross was hoisted up high. "You said you're the Son of God—so save yourself!"

As the two criminals were raised on crosses either side of Jesus, one sneered, "Yes, save yourself and save us too!"

"How dare you!" the second thief groaned. "We deserve this, but Jesus is innocent. Lord, remember me when you reach your kingdom."

"I promise you," whispered Jesus, "today

you will be with me in paradise."

Even though it was midday, darkness suddenly fell over the land. Close by at the foot of the cross, was Jesus' heartbroken mother, and His close friends including John, Mary Magdalene, and Salome.

"Mother, take care of John as if he were your own son," Jesus murmered. "John, look after my mother as if she were your own."

Jesus hung in agony on the cross for three long hours. Then He lifted His head and cried aloud, "My God! Why have you abandoned me?" Somebody rushed to lift a stick with a sponge on the end that had been dipped in wine so He could have a drink. Jesus cried out again, "Father, I give up my spirit into your hands. It is finished."

And His head drooped.

At that very moment, the earth rumbled and shook, and rocks split open. People said that the great curtain in the temple ripped from top to bottom. Others said they saw graves open and spirits rise from them.

A Roman officer at the foot of the cross looked up and gasped, "This man truly was the Son of God."

Matthew chapter 27; Mark chapter 15; Luke chapter 23; John chapter 19

The First Easter

The evening after Jesus had been put to death, a wealthy Jew called Joseph of Arimathea begged Pontius Pilate to allow him to bury Jesus' body. Pilate agreed. So Joseph went with his friend, Nicodemus, back to Golgotha, where women were still weeping at the foot of His cross. Gently,

Joseph and Nicodemus lifted Jesus' poor, bleeding body down. They wrapped Him in a linen shroud with burial spices and, accompanied by the sobbing women, took Him to a nearby cemetery. There the two men laid Jesus in a small, cavelike tomb that Joseph had already paid for, and rolled a heavy stone across the entrance. Full of grief and with nothing else to do, they left.

Meanwhile, some Jewish officials had been to see Pilate. "Jesus of Nazareth said He would rise up again after three days," they told the Roman governor. "Have soldiers guard His tomb so no one can steal the body, then tell everyone that He's miraculously come back to life." Pilate nodded and sent the men away.

Pilate's guards sat outside Jesus' tomb through the night of that first Good Friday—nothing happened. They kept watch all the next day and again nobody came. But as dawn broke on the Sabbath, the third day, the earth suddenly shook so violently that it knocked the soldiers off their feet. A white light blazed out of the sky and shone over the tomb. Through the glare, the terrified soldiers watched the glowing figure of a man roll away the massive stone from the tomb entrance. The soldiers were scared by what they saw and fled for their lives.

Not long afterward a group of grieving women arrived at the cemetery to pay their respects at the tomb. They included Jesus'

friends Mary Magdalene, Mary the mother
of James and John, Salome, and Joanna.
When they saw that the soldiers were gone
and the stone had been rolled
away, they screamed in
horror. Someone must
have stolen
Jesus' body!
Inside the tomb
where Jesus' body
should have been,
two shining figures
were sitting. "Why
are you looking for
the living among the dead?" the figures
said. "Don't you remember that the Son of
Man said He would rise on the third day?"

Mary Magdalene raced to fetch the disciples Peter and John. When the two men saw the empty tomb they were full of anger. They went off to try to find out who had taken the body. Mary sank down outside the tomb, sobbing. Then suddenly she sensed someone behind her. Mary spun round and, through her tears she saw a blurry figure whom she thought must be the cemetery gardener. "Why are you weeping?" the man asked.

"If you moved the body," she begged, "please tell me where to."

The man said just one word.

"Mary."

Mary's heart stood still. Suddenly, she recognized the man—it was Jesus!

"Go now," Jesus said softly, as Mary fell at His feet, gazing up at Him in wonder. "Find the disciples and tell them that I will soon be returning to my Father."

Meanwhile, the other women who had seen the empty tomb were hurrying homeward when all at once, a man appeared out of nowhere on the road in front of them. "Good morning," He said.

The women were amazed and couldn't believe who they were hearing and seeing.

"Don't be afraid," Jesus said. "Go and tell my disciples to travel to Galilee and I will meet them there soon."

Matthew chapters 27, 28; Mark chapter 16; Luke chapters 23, 24; John chapters 19, 20

Jesus and Doubting Thomas

Late morning on the third day after Jesus' death, Mary Magdalene burst into the room where the grieving disciples sat together. "I have seen Jesus!" she cried, flushed with excitement, and told them everything that had happened at the tomb. But as much as the disciples wanted to believe her, they couldn't.

Meanwhile, two of Jesus' disciples were
on their way from Jerusalem to the nearby
village of Emmaus. As they walked with
heavy hearts, a stranger joined them and
began talking. To the disciples'
astonishment, the stranger didn't seem to
have heard anything of the events everyone
was talking about—the death of Jesus and
the disappearance of His body. However, he
seemed to know the ancient holy writings
very well and began explaining them.

"Don't you know that the holy men of
old said that the Messiah would have to
suffer to win glory?"

Later on the disciples shared a meal with
the stranger and he blessed some bread,

broke it into pieces, and gave it to them. It was only then that they realized who he really was. "Jesus!" they gasped in astonishment. And at that moment, He disappeared.

The disciples hurried back to the city and went straight to tell the others—only to find that Jesus had appeared to Peter too!

Everyone began talking at once, full of excitement and asking to hear the stories again and again. No one noticed the newcomer arrive in their midst.

"Peace be with you," said Jesus, as everyone stood back in fear as though He was a ghost. "Don't be frightened," He said, "it's me. Look—here are the wounds on my hands and feet."

But one disciple was missing—Thomas. When his friends told him what had happened he didn't believe it. Eight days later everyone was gathered again to talk and pray. Halfway through the meeting, Jesus appeared once more. "See for yourself, Thomas," He said. "Come and touch my wounds. Have faith—it's true."

Thomas broke down. "My Lord, it's really you," he sobbed. "Bless you for believing," Jesus said gently. "But even more blessed are those who won't see me and yet will still believe."

Matthew chapter 28; Mark chapter 16; Luke chapter 24; John chapter 20

The Stranger on the Beach

One evening, some of the disciples gathered at the Sea of Galilee. Peter wanted to take a little boat out and go fishing, just as he used to do in the days when he was a fisherman. Soon he and his friends, including James, John, Thomas, and Nathaniel, were sailing out into open waters under a starry sky. How free and peaceful it felt—a welcome relief from the terrible events in the city in recent weeks.

All night, the disciples waited for fish to fill their nets, but when dawn came, they were all empty.

Then a voice floated across the waves. "Have you caught anything?"

Peering into the distance, the disciples could see the figure of a man on the shore.

"No, nothing." they yelled back.

"Try dropping your nets to the right side of the boat," came the voice.

The disciples thought it was worth a try. They soon felt their nets become heavy and they could hardly lift them.

Peter, James, and John looked at each

other and they remembered a time in the
past when exactly the same thing had
    happened. "It's Jesus!" they exclaimed.
        Peter couldn't wait to finish hauling
in the catch and sail to shore, so he
dived straight into the water and
swam to be the first to reach Jesus.
        Before long, Peter and the rest of
                            the friends joined
                            Jesus on the
                            shore, and
                        gathered around a
            little fire on the beach.
They sat roasting fish for breakfast, and it
was just like old times.

John chapter 21

The Ascension
into Heaven

It was finally time for Jesus to leave the world for good. He gathered his disciples together and walked to the Mount of Olives, a short way from Jerusalem.

"Stay in the city for a while," Jesus told His eleven old friends. "You have already all been baptized once—by John the Baptist, with water. But soon you will all be baptized again—this time with the Holy Spirit. God is going to send you powerful gifts and I want you to use them by going out into the world and telling people in every country about me. Baptize all those who believe in me as my followers, in the name of the Father, the Son and the Holy Spirit. Teach them everything that I have taught you." Jesus looked at His friends' worried faces. "Don't forget," He said gently, "I will be with you always, until the end of time."

With that, Jesus rose up into the air, higher and higher, until He disappeared into a blazing cloud of glory.

As the disciples squinted up at the

dazzling light, it glimmered, gleamed, and then faded… Jesus was gone but they carried on gazing up at the empty blue sky.

"Men of Galilee, what are you looking at?" came a voice. The disciples turned to find two men in glowing robes standing next to them.

"Jesus has gone, but one day He will come back to you in the same way."

Full of wonder and sadness, the disciples were comforted and made their way back to Jerusalem. They knew they would not see Jesus again soon, but were sure that one day He would return in glory.

Matthew chapter 28; Mark chapter 16; Luke chapter 24; Acts chapter 1

The Coming of the Holy Spirit

The disciples were in Jerusalem waiting for the Holy Spirit to come and baptize them, as Jesus had told them. Meanwhile they decided to replace the traitor, Judas Iscariot, with a new disciple. Then they would be twelve once more, as Jesus had originally intended. They prayed for guidance, and cast votes, and Matthias was chosen. The twelve became known as the apostles. Then the waiting continued.

Fifty days after Passover and the death of Jesus, it was the feast of Pentecost—when Jews celebrated how God had given their religious laws to Moses. The apostles were celebrating the feast, when suddenly a mighty sound like a rushing wind filled their ears as though it was all around them in the house. The apostles felt alive and full of energy, and turning to each other in astonishment, they saw that every man had a tiny flame hovering over his head.

"It must be the Holy Spirit!" they cried, and they found they were all speaking in different languages.

Realizing they had been blessed with the special gifts Jesus had talked about, the apostles excitedly ran out into the streets. Some found themselves giving thanks to God in Greek. Others were preaching about Jesus in Latin. Some were praising the Holy Spirit in Arabic, and many other languages.

Worshipers from foreign lands had come to Jerusalem for Pentecost and they were stunned. "These men are from Galilee!" they marveled. "How can they speak our language?"

However, some people just laughed and said that the apostles were drunk.

Then Peter began preaching and everyone who heard him was stirred by his passion. "We are not drunk," he laughed. "We are followers of Jesus of Nazareth. He has risen from the dead, we have seen it with our own eyes. Today we have been blessed by the Holy Spirit with these gifts of languages. Anyone who is truly sorry for their sins and follows the teachings of Jesus will be blessed too. Who wants to join us?"

That day the apostles baptized over three thousand people as followers of Jesus. The foundations of the Christian Church had been laid.

Acts chapters 1, 2